Keep Your Mind Fit

THIS IS A CARLTON BOOK

This edition published in 2007 by
Carlton Books
20 Mortimer Street
London W1T 3JW

ISBN: 978-1-84442-510-5

Printed in Dubai

The puzzles in this book previously appeared in
Mensa Puzzle Challenge and *Mensa Puzzle Challenge 2*

Keep Your
Mind
Fit

CARLTON

WHAT IS MENSA?

Mensa is the international society for people with a high IQ.
We have more than 100,000 members in over 40 countries worldwide.

The society's aims are:
>   to identify and foster human intelligence for the benefit of humanity
>   to encourage research in the nature, characteristics, and uses of intelligence
>   to provide a stimulating intellectual and social environment for its members

Anyone with an IQ score in the top two per cent of population is eligible to become a member of Mensa – are you the 'one in 50' we've been looking for?

Mensa membership offers an excellent range of benefits:
>   Networking and social activities nationally and around the world
>   Special Interest Groups – hundreds of chances to pursue your hobbies
>   and interests – from art to zoology!
>   Monthly members' magazine and regional newsletters
>   Local meetings – from games challenges to food and drink
>   National and international weekend gatherings and conferences
>   Intellectually stimulating lectures and seminars
>   Access to the worldwide SIGHT network for travellers and hosts

For more information about Mensa: www.mensa.org, or

British Mensa Ltd.,
St John's House,
St John's Square,
Wolverhampton
WV2 4AH
Telephone: +44 (0) 1902 772771
E-mail: enquiries@mensa.org.uk
www.mensa.org.uk

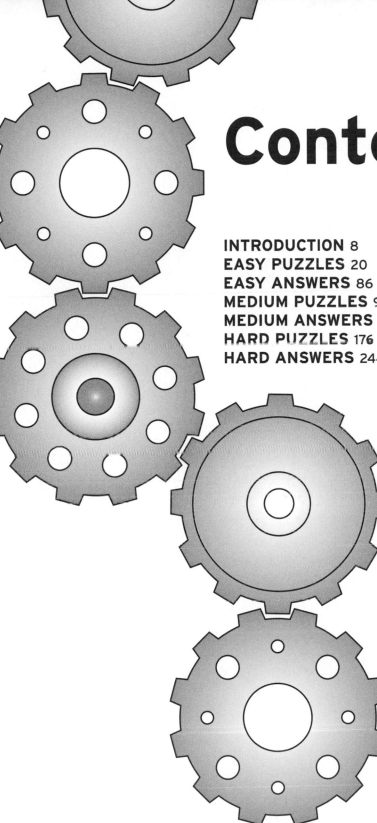

Contents

Introduction:
The Puzzle Reflex
by Tim Dedopulos

Puzzles are as old as humankind. It's inevitable – it's the way we think. Our brains make sense of the world around us by looking at the pieces that combine to make up our environment. Each piece is then compared to everything else we have encountered. We compare it by shape, size, colour, textures, a thousand different qualities, and place it into the mental categories it seems to belong to. Then also consider other nearby objects, and examine what we know about them, to give context. We keep on following this web of connections until we have enough understanding of the object of our attention to allow us to proceed in the current situation. We may never have seen a larch before, but we can still identify it as a tree. Most of the time, just basic recognition is good enough, but every time we perceive an object, it is cross-referenced, analysed, pinned down – puzzled out.

This capacity for logical analysis – for reason – is one of the greatest tools in our mental arsenal, on a par with creativity and lateral induction. Without it, science would be non-existent, and mathematics no more than a shorthand for counting items. In fact, although we might have made it out of the caves, we wouldn't have got far.

Furthermore, we automatically compare ourselves to each other – we place ourselves in mental boxes along with everything else. We like to know where we stand. It gives us an instinctive urge to compete, both against our previous bests and against each other. Experience, flexibility and strength are acquired through pushing personal boundaries, and that's as true of the mind as it is of the body. Deduction is something that we derive satisfaction and worth from, part of the complex blend of factors that goes into making up our self-image. We get a very pleasurable sense of achievement from succeeding at something, particularly if we suspected it might be too hard for us.

The brain gives meaning and structure to the world through analysis, pattern recognition, and logical deduction – and our urge to measure and test ourselves is an unavoidable reflex that results from that. So what could be more natural than spending time puzzling?

EARLY PUZZLES

The urge to solve puzzles appears to be a universal human constant. They can be found in every culture, and in every time that we have good archaeological evidence for. The earliest material uncovered so far that is indisputably a puzzle has been dated to a little after 2000BC – and the first true writing we know of only dates back to 2600BC. The puzzle text is recorded on a writing tablet, preserved from ancient Babylonia. It is a mathematical puzzle based around working out the sides of a triangle.

Other puzzles from around the same time have also been discovered. The Rhind Papyrus from ancient Egypt describes a puzzle that is almost certainly a precursor of the traditional English riddle "As I Was Going to St. Ives." In the Rhind Papyrus, a puzzle is constructed around the clearly unreal situation of seven houses, each containing seven cats – and every cat kills seven mice that themselves had each consumed seven ears of millet.

In a similar foreshadowing, a set of very early puzzle jugs – Phoenician work from around 1700BC, found in Cyprus – echo designs that were to become popular in medieval Europe. These particular jugs, belonging to a broad category known as Askoi, had to be filled from the bottom. This form of trick vessel would later become known as a Cadogan Teapot. These devices have no lid, and have to be filled through a hole in the base. Because the hole funnels to a point inside the vessel, it can be filled to about half-way without spilling when it is turned back upright.

Earlier finds do exist, but so much context is lost down through the years that it can be difficult to be certain that the creators were thinking of puzzles specifically, or just of mathematical demonstrations. A set of ancient Babylonian tablets showing geometric progressions – mathematical sequences – is thought to be from 2300BC. One of the very first mathematical finds though, thought to possibly be from as far back as 2700 BC, is a set of stone balls carved into the shapes of the Platonic solids. These are regular convex polyhedrons – three-dimensional solid shapes made up solely of identical regular polygons. The most familiar is the basic cube, made up of six squares, but there are just four others – the tetrahedron, made up of four equilateral triangles; the octahedron, made up of eight equilateral triangles; the dodecahedron, made from twelve pentagons, and the icosahedron, made of twenty equilateral triangles.

There's no way now of knowing whether the carvings were teaching aids, puzzle or game tools, demonstrations of a theory, artistic constructions or even religious icons. The fact they exist at all however shows that someone had previously spent time working out a significant abstract mathematical puzzle – discovering which regular convex polyhedrons could exist.

AMENEMHET'S LABYRINTH

One of the greatest physical puzzles ever engineered comes from the same time period. The Egyptian Pharaoh Amenemhet III constructed a funerary pyramid with a huge temple complex around it in the form of an incredible labyrinth. Designed to guard the Pharaoh's mummy and treasures from disturbance or robbery, the labyrinth was so lavish and cunning that it is said to have been both the inspiration and template for the famous labyrinth that Daedalus built at Knossos for King Minos of Crete – the one that supposedly contained the Minotaur.

PUZZLE HISTORY

Coming forward in time, the evidence for the variety and complexity of puzzles gets ever stronger – an inevitable fact of archaeological and historical research. Greek legend claims that numbered dice were invented at the siege of Troy around 1200BC. We know that there was a craze for lateral thinking puzzles and logical dilemmas in the Greek culture from the 5th to 3rd centuries BC. A lot of very important mathematical work also took place in Greece from the middle of the first millennium BC, moving across to Rome during the first centuries AD. At the same time, the Chinese were playing with numerical puzzles and oddities, most famously the magic square, which they called *Lo Shu* (River Map), and also doing more strong mathematical work.

Puzzles and puzzle-like games that survive through to modern times get more common as we get closer to modern times, naturally. The game of Go arose in China some time around 500 BC, spreading to Japan a thousand years later – it is still an important sport there. At the same time, Chess was first appearing, either in India (*Chaturanga*), China (*Xiang-qi*), or both. Puzzle rings that you have to find out how to separate also appeared in China, possibly in the 3rd century AD, as did Snakes & Ladders, around 700AD.

The first known reference to a game played with cards is in 969AD, in records reporting the activities of the Chinese Emperor Mu-tsung. These are not thought to be the playing cards now familiar in the west, however – it seems likely that those arose in Persia during the 11th or 12th century AD. The physical puzzle Solitaire is first reported in 1697AD. As the eighteenth century gave way to the nineteenth, the forces of the industrial revolution really started to transform the way that ideas propagated, and the puzzle world exploded. Some of the more notable highlights include the invention of the jigsaw puzzle by John Spilsbury in 1767; Tic-Tac-Toe's first formal discussion in 1820, by Charles Babbage; poker first appearing around 1830 in the USA; Lucas inventing the Tower of Hanoi puzzle in 1883; the first crossword appearing in New York World on December 21, 1913, created by Arthur Wynne; Erno Rubik's invention of his Cube in 1974; and the invention of Sudoku in 1979 for Dell Magazines by Howard Garns, an American, who first called it "Number Place".

PLASTICITY

It turns out that it's a good thing puzzles are such an important part of the human psyche. Recent advances in the scientific fields of neurology and cognitive psychology have hammered home the significance of puzzles and mental exercise like never before.

We now understand that the brain continually builds, shapes and organises itself all through our lives. It is the only organ to be able to do so. Previously, we had assumed that the brain was constructed to optimise infant development, but the truth is that it continually rewrites its own operating instructions. It can route around physical damage, maximise its efficiency in dealing with commonly encountered situations and procedures, and alter its very structure in response to our experiences. This incredible flexibility is referred to as plasticity.

The most important implication of plasticity is that our mental abilities and cognitive fitness can be exercised at any age. Just like the muscles of the body, our minds can respond to exercise, allowing us to be more retentive and mentally fitter. Our early lives are the most important time, of course. Infants develop almost twice as many synapses

– the mental connections that are the building-blocks of the mind – as we retain as adults, to make sure that every experience can be learnt from and given its own space in the developing mental structure. The first thirty-six months are particularly vital, the ones which will shape the patterns of our intellect, character and socialisation for life. A good education through to adulthood – stretching the brain right through childhood – is one of the strongest indicators of late-life mental health, particularly when followed with a mentally challenging working life.

Just as importantly however, there is little difference between the brain at the age of 25 and the age of 75. As time passes, the brain optimises itself for the lifestyle we feed it. Circuits that are hardly ever used get re-adapted to offer greater efficiency in tasks we regularly use. Just as our body maximises available energy by removing muscle we don't use, the brain removes mental tone we're never stretching – and in the same way that working out can build up muscle, so mental exercise can restore a "fit" mind.

PUZZLE SOLVING AND BRAIN GROWTH

A surprising amount of mental decline in elders is now thought to be down to insufficient mental exercise. Where severe mental decline occurs, it is usually linked to the tissue damage of Alzheimer's Disease – although there is now even evidence that strong mental exercise lets the brain route around even Alzheimer's damage, lessening impairment. In other cases, where there is no organic damage, the main cause is disuse. Despite old assumptions, we do not significantly lose huge swathes of brain cells as we age. Better still, mental strength that has been allowed to atrophy may be rebuilt.

Research projects across the world have discovered strong patterns linking highly lucid venerable people. These include above-average education, acceptance of change, satisfying personal accomplishments, physical exercise, a clever spouse, and a strong engagement with life, including reading, social activity, travel, keeping up with new ideas, and regularly solving puzzles. Not all the things we assume to be engagement are actually helpful, however. Useful intellectual pursuits are the actively stimulating ones – such as solving jigsaws, crosswords and other puzzles, playing chess, and reading books that stimulate the imagination or require some mental effort to properly digest. However, passive intellectual pursuits may actually hasten the mind's decay. Watching television is the most damaging such pastime, but surprisingly anything that makes you "switch off" mentally can also be harmful, such as listening to certain types of music, reading very low-content magazines and even getting most of your social exposure on the telephone. For social interaction to be helpful, it may really need to be face to face.

THE COLUMBIA STUDY

A team of researchers from Columbia University in New York tracked more than 1,750 pensioners from the northern Manhattan region over a period of seven years. The subjects underwent periodic medical and psychological examination to assess both their mental health and the physical condition of their brains. Participants also provided the researchers with detailed information regarding their daily activities. The study found that even when you remove education and career attainment from the equation, leisure activity significantly reduced the risk of dementia.

The study's author, Dr Yaakov Stern, found that "Even when controlling for factors like ethnic group, education and occupation, subjects with high leisure activity had 38% less risk of developing dementia." Activities were broken into three categories: physical, social and intellectual. Each one was found to be beneficial, but the greatest protection came from intellectual pursuits. The more activity, the greater the protection – the cumulative benefit of each separate leisure pursuit was found to be 8%. Stern also found that leisure activity helped to prevent the physical damage caused by Alzheimer's from actually manifesting as dementia:

> "Our study suggests that aspects of life experience supply a set of skills or repertoires that allow an individual to cope with progressing Alzheimer's Disease pathology for a longer time before the disease becomes clinically apparent. Maintaining intellectual and social engagement through participation in everyday activities seems to buffer healthy individuals against cognitive decline in later life."

STAYING LUCID

There is strong evidence to back Stern's conclusion. Dr David Bennett of the Rush Alzheimer's Disease Centre in Chicago led a study that evaluated a group of venerable participants on a yearly basis, and then after death examined their donated brains for signs of Alzheimer's. The participants all led active lives mentally, socially and physically, and none of them suffered from dementia at the time of their death. It was discovered that more than a third of the participants had sufficient brain-tissue damage to warrant diagnosis of Alzheimer's Disease, including serious lesions in the brain tissue. This group *had* recorded lower scores than other participants in episodic memory tests – remembering story episodes, for example – but performed identically in cognitive function and reasoning tests. A similar study took place with the aid of the nuns of the Order of the School Sisters of Notre Dame. The Order boasts a long average lifespan – 85 years – and came to the attention of researchers when it became clear that its members did not seem to suffer from any dementia either. The distinguishing key about the Order is that the nuns shun idleness and mental vacuity, taking particular effort to remain mentally active. All sorts of pursuits are encouraged, such as solving puzzles, playing challenging games, writing, holding seminars on current affairs, knitting and engaging with local government. As before, there was plenty of evidence of the physical damage associated with Alzheimer's Disease, but none of the mental damage that usually accompanied it, even in some nonagenarian participants.

MENTAL REPAIR

Other studies have also tried to enumerate the benefits of mental activity. A massive group study led by Michael Valenzuela from the University of New South Wales' School of Psychiatry tracked data from almost 30,000 people worldwide. The results were clear – as well as indicating the same clear relationship previously found between schooling, career and mental health, people of all backgrounds whose daily lives include a high degree of mental stimulation are 46% less likely to suffer dementia. This holds true even for people who take up mentally challenging activities as they get older – if you use your mind, the brain still adapts to protect it. If you do not use it, the brain lets it falter.

PUZZLE SOLVING TECHNIQUES

Puzzle solving is more of an art than a science. It requires mental flexibility, a little understanding of the underlying principles and possibilities, and sometimes a little intuition. It is often said of crosswords that you have to learn the writer's style to get really good at his or her puzzles, but the same thing applies to most other puzzle types to a certain extent, and that includes the many and various kinds you'll find in this book.

SEQUENCE PUZZLES

Sequence puzzles challenge you to find a missing value or item, or to complete a pattern according to the correct underlying design. In this type of puzzle, you are provided with enough previous entries in the sequence that the underlying logic can be worked out. Once the sequence is understood, the missing entry can be calculated. When the patterns are simple, the sequence will be readily visible to the naked eye. It is not hard to figure out that the next term in the sequence 1, 2, 4, 8, 16, ? is going to be a further doubling to 32. Numerical sequences are just the expression of a mathematical formula however, and can therefore get almost infinitely complex.

Proper recreational puzzles stay firmly within the bounds of human ability, of course. With the more complex puzzles, the best approach is often to calculate the differences between successive terms in the sequences, and look for patterns in the way that those differences are changing. You should also be aware that in some puzzles, the terms of a sequence may not necessarily represent single items. Different parts or digits of each term may progress according to different calculations. For example, the sequence 921, 642, 383, 164 is actually three simple sequences stuck together - 9, 6, 2, 0 ; 2, 4, 8, 16; and 1, 2, 3, 4. The next term will be - 3325. Alternatively, in puzzles where the sequence terms are given as times, they may actually just represent the times they depict, but they might also be literal numbers, or pairs of numbers to be treated as totally different sequences, or even require conversion from hours: minutes to just minutes before the sequence becomes apparent.

For example, 11:14 in a puzzle might represent the time 11:14, or perhaps the time 23:14 - or the numbers 11 and 14, the numbers 23 and 14, the number 1114, the number 2314, or even the number 674 (11 * 60 minutes, with the remaining 14 minutes also added). As you can see, solving sequence puzzles requires a certain amount of trial and error as you test difference possibilities, as well as a degree of lateral thinking. It would be a very harsh puzzle setter who expected you to guess some sort of sequence out of context however. So in the absence of a clue

otherwise, 11:14 would be highly unlikely to represent 11 months and 14 days, or the value 11 in base 14, or even 11 hours and 14 minutes converted to seconds - unless it was given as 11:14:00, of course.

Letter-based sequences are all representational of course, as unlike numbers, letters have no underlying structure save as symbols. Once you deduce what the letters represent, the answer can be obvious. The sequence D, N, O, ? may seem abstract, until you think of months of the year in reverse order.

In visual sequences - such as pattern grids - the sequence will always be there for you to see, and your task is to look for repeating patterns. As with number sequences, easy grids can be immediately apparent. In harder puzzles, the sequences can become significantly long, and often be presented in ways that make them difficult to identify. Puzzle setters love to start grids of this type from the bottom right-hand square, and then progress in spirals or in a back-and-forth pattern - sometimes even diagonally.

Odd-one-out problems are a specialised case of sequence pattern where you are given the elements of a sequence or related set, along with one item that breaks the sequence. Like other sequence puzzles, these can range from very easy to the near-impossible. Spotting the odd one in 2, 4, 6, 7, 8 is trivial. It would be almost impossible to guess the odd item from the set of B, F,

H, N, O unless you already knew that the set in question was the physical elements on the second row of the standard periodic table. Even then, you might need a copy of the periodic table itself to notice that hydrogen, H, is on the first row. As with any other sequence problem, any odd-one-out should contain enough information in the puzzle, accompanying text and title to set the context for finding the correct answer. In the above case, a puzzle title along the lines of "An Elementary Puzzle" would probably be sufficient to make it fair game.

EQUATION PUZZLES

Equation puzzles are similar to sequences, but require a slightly different methodology. In these problems, you are given a set of mathematical calculations that contain one or more unknown terms. These may be represented as equations, as in the traditional form of $2x + 3y = 9$, or they may be presented visually, for example as two anvils and three iron bars on one side of a scale and nine horseshoes balancing on the other side of the scale. For each Unknown – x, y, anvils, etc – you need one equation or other set of values before you can calculate a definitive answer. If these are lacking, you cannot get the problem down to just one possible solution. Take the equation above, $2x + 3y = 9$. There are two unknowns, and therefore many

answers. For example, x can be 3 and y can be 1 – for x, $2 * 3 = 6$; for y, $3 * 1 = 3$, and overall, $6 + 3 = 9$ – but x can also be 1.5 and y can be 2... and an infinite range of other possibilities. So when solving equation puzzles, you need to consider all the equations together before you can solve the problem.

To return to our example equation above, if you *also* knew that $x + 2y = 7$, you could then begin to solve the puzzle. The key with equation problems is to get your equation down to containing just one unknown term, which then lets you get a value for that term, and in turn lets you get the value of the other unknown/s. So, for example, in our previous equations ($2x + 3y = 9$ and $x + 2y = 7$) you could manipulate one equation to work out what x actually represents in terms of y ("How many Y is each X?") in one equation, and then replace the x in the other equation with it's value in y, to get a calculation that just has y as the sole unknown factor. It's not as confusing as it sounds so long as you take it step by step:

We know that

$x + 2y = 7$

Any change made to both sides of an equation balances out, and so doesn't change the truth of the equation. For example, consider $2 + 2 = 4$. If you add 1 to each side, the equation is still true. That is, $2 + 2 + 1 = 4 + 1$. We can use this cancelling out to get x and y on opposite sides of the equation, which will let us represent x in terms of y:

x + 2y - 2y = 7 - 2y.

Now the + 2y - 2y cancels out:

x = 7 - 2y.

Now we know x is a way of saying "7-2y", we can replace it in the other equation.

2x + 3y = 9 becomes:

2 * (7 - 2y) + 3y = 9.

Note 2x means that x is in the equation twice, so our way of re-writing x as y needs to be doubled to stay accurate. Expanding that out:

(2 * 7) - (2 * 2y) + 3y = 9, or

14 - 4y + 3y = 9.

The next step is to get just amounts of y on one side, and numbers on the other.

14 - 4y + 3y - 14 = 9 - 14.

In other words,

-4y + 3y = -5.

Now, -4 + 3 is -1, so:

-y = -5, and that means y=5.

Now you can go back to the first equation, x + 2y = 7, and replace y to find x.

x + (2 * 5) = 7

x + 10 = 7

x + 10 - 10 = 7 - 10

x = 7 - 10

and, finally.

x = -3.

As a last step, test your equations by replacing your number values for x and y in both at the same time, and making sure they balance correctly.

2x + 3y = 9 and x + 2y = 7.

(2 * -3) + (3 * 5) = 9 and -3 + (2 * 5) = 7

(-6 + 15) = 9; and (-3 + 10) = 7.

9 = 9 and 7 = 7.

The answers are correct. Any equation-based puzzle you're presented with will contain enough information for you to work out the solution. If more than two terms are unknown, the technique is to use one equation to find one unknown as a value of the others, and then replace it in all the other equations. That gives you a new set of equations containing one less unknown term. You then repeat the process of working out an unknown again, until you finally get down to one unknown term and its numerical value. Then you replace the term you now know with its value in the equations for the level above to get the next term, and continue back on up like that. It's like a mathematical version of the old wooden Towers of Hanoi puzzle. As a final tip, remember that you should have one equation per unknown term, and that if one of your unknown variables is missing from an equation, the equation can be said to have 0 of that variable on either or both sides. That is, 4y + 2z = 8 is the same as 0x + 4y + 2z = 8.

Happy puzzling!

REFERENCES

Chronology of Recreational Mathematics; David Singmaster; http://www.eldar.org/~problemi/singmast/recchron.html

Pythagoras's theorem in Babylonian mathematics; J J O'Connor and E F Robertson; http://www-history.mcs.st-andrews.ac.uk/HistTopics/Babylonian_Pythagoras.html

The Rhind Mathematical Papyrus; http://en.wikipedia.org/wiki/Rhind_Mathematical_Papyrus

Puzzle Jug; http://en.wikipedia.org/wiki/Puzzle_jug

The Egyptian Labyrinth; http://www.amazeingart.com/seven-wonders/egyptian-labyrinth.html

The Ancient Egyptian Labyrinth; http://www.catchpenny.org/labyrin.html

Alzheimer's: Prevention, Treatment, and Slowing Down; Doug Russell, Jeanne Segal and Monika White; http://www.helpguide.org/elder/alzheimers_prevention_slowing_down_treatment.htm

The Human Brain; http://www.fi.edu/brain/exercise.htm

Power Up Your Brain; Terri Needels & Toby Bilanow; http://health.msn.com/guides/agingwell/articlepage.aspx?cp-documentid=100143902

Keeping Your Brain Fit For Life; Katherine Kam; http://www.positscience.com/newsroom/news/news/111406.php

Preliminary Results from PopCap Games and Games for Health; Peter Smith; http://www.gamesforhealth.org/archives/000125.html

Older Game Players Derive Mental Workouts, Stress Relief and Pain Distraction from Playing; Garth Chouteau; http://www.popcap.com/press/index.php?page=press_releases&release=survey_seniors_10-4-06

Complex Brain Circuits May Protect Against Alzheimer's; Susan Conova; http://www.cumc.columbia.edu/news/in-vivo/Vol3_Iss11_nov_dec_04/index.html

Use It or Lose It?; Beth Azar; http://www.apa.org/monitor/may02/useit.html

Fight Alzheimer's With an Active Brain; http://www.msnbc.msn.com/id/8292945

Want a Sharp Mind for your Golden Years? Start Now; Marilyn Elias; http://www.bri.ucla.edu/bri_weekly/news_050818.asp

How to Prevent Alzheimer's; http://www.sixwise.com/newsletters/05/08/24/how_to_prevent_alzheimers_the_most_effective_ways_to_avoid_this_rapidly_increasing_disease.htm

Lifestyle May Be Key to Slowing Brain's Aging; Rob Stein; http://www.washingtonpost.com/wp-dyn/content/article/2005/08/13/AR2005081300855.html

Disorder May Precede Alzheimer's; John Fauber; http://www.findarticles.com/p/articles/mi_qn4196/is_20050308/ai_n12411071

Mental Activities May Reduce Alzheimer's Risk; http://www.kirotv.com/health/1232090/detail.html

Brain Savers; A. J. Mann; http://www.time.com/time/magazine/article/0,9171,1002535,00.html?internalid=ACA

Building a Better Brain; Daniel Golden & Alexander Tsiaras; http://www.enchantedmind.com/html/science/build_better_brain.html

The Nuns Who Won't Sit Still; Marge Engelmann; http://www.agenet.com/Category_Pages/document_display.asp?Id=12561&

Mental Exercise Nearly Halves Risk of Dementia; http://www.livescience.com/humanbiology/060125_delay_dementia.html

Use Your Brain, Halve Your Risk of Dementia; Susi Hamilton; http://www.unsw.edu.au/news/pad/articles/2006/jan/Dementia_brain_reserve.html

14-Day Health Plan Improves Memory; http://www.livescience.com/humanbiology/051213_memory_exercise.html

The Happiness Manifesto; http://www.uofapain.med.ualberta.ca/documents/manifesto1.pdf

Can We Live Happily Ever After?; Ron Horvath; http://www.australianreview.net/digest/2006/10/horvath.html

Simple Lifestyle Changes May Improve Cognitive Function; http://www.news-medical.net/?id=18102

Effects of Self-Esteem on Age-Related Changes in Cognition; Sonia Lupien, Jens Pruessner, Catherine Lord and Michael Meaney; http://www.annalsnyas.org/cgi/content/full/1032/1/186

Low Self-Esteem 'Shrinks Brain'; Pallab Ghosh; http://news.bbc.co.uk/2/hi/health/3224674.stm

Easy Puzzles

If solving puzzles is a pleasurable activity – and all the evidence that we have suggests that it most certainly is – then this is the section that will let you sharpen your knife in preparation for the feast. The puzzles here represent the same types of problem that you'll find throughout this book. They'll certainly get you thinking, but not too hard – the answers to these problems are reassuringly straightforward, and you may find that many of them are readily apparent.

Don't get complacent, however. As well as warming up your mind for the challenges to come, this section also gives you an important chance to get used to the way that the puzzles work. You'll start to get a feeling for the way that the puzzle authors are thinking, and you'll also pick up a good intuitive grounding in the particular vagaries of the different puzzle types.

If you're new to puzzles, then it's probably going to be best for you to work your way through this entire section before moving on to the next one. Get a firm victory under your belt – and remember to pat yourself on the back – before moving on to some of the harsher problems. If you're more experienced in the ways of puzzling, you might prefer to dip into this section to warm yourself up, starting each of your puzzle sessions with a few of the problems here to get your brain in gear.

Whichever way you approach these problems however, remember one critical thing – to have fun!

Which of these groups of triangles is the odd one out?

Answer see page **88**

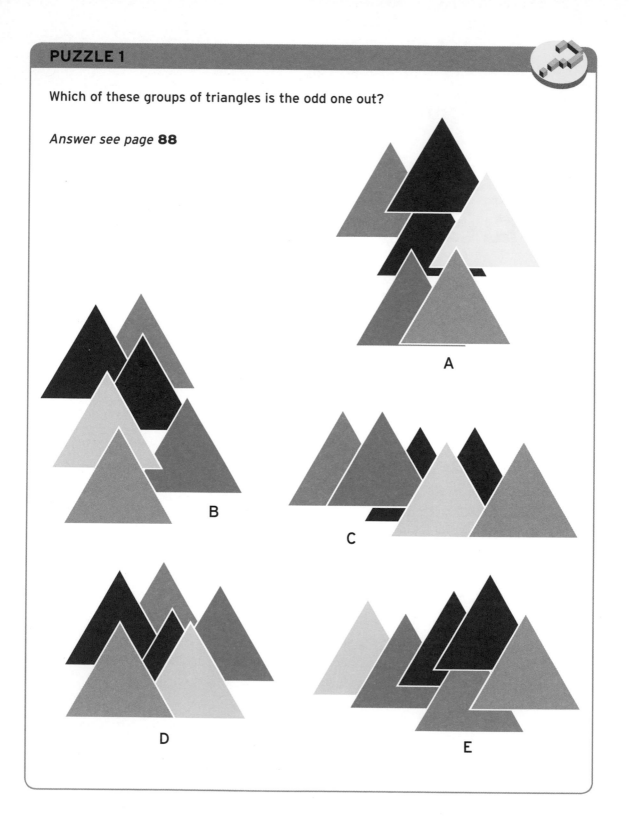

A

B

C

D

E

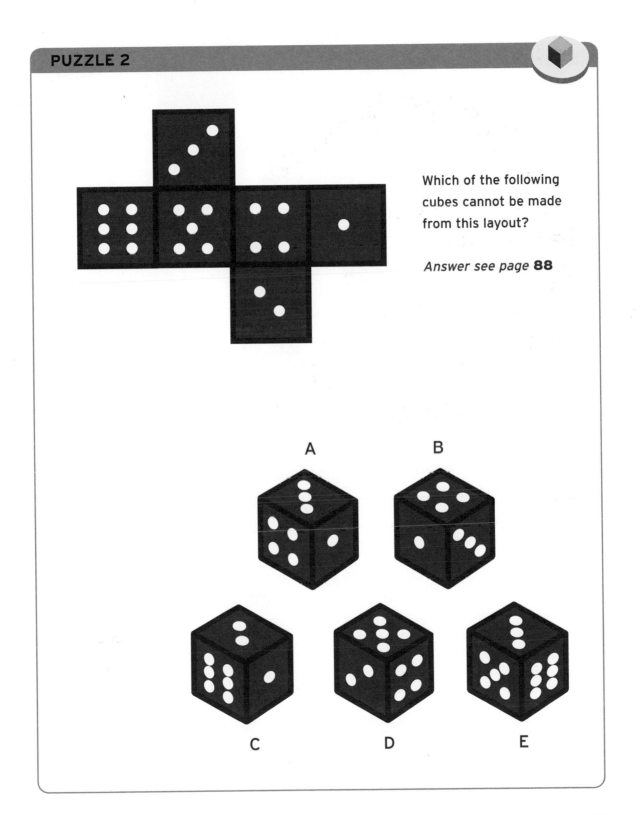

Which of the following cubes cannot be made from this layout?

Answer see page **88**

A

B

C

D

E

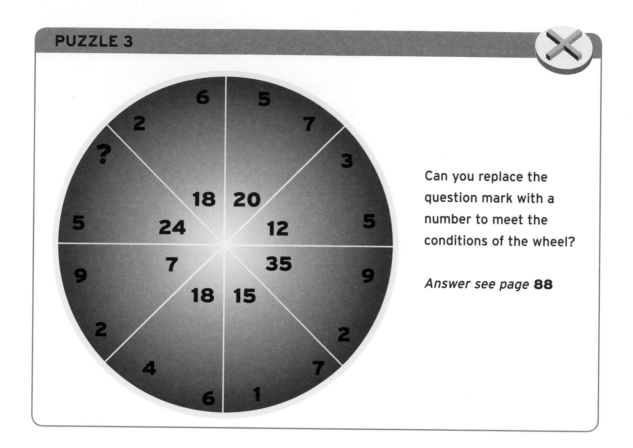

Can you replace the question mark with a number to meet the conditions of the wheel?

*Answer see page **88***

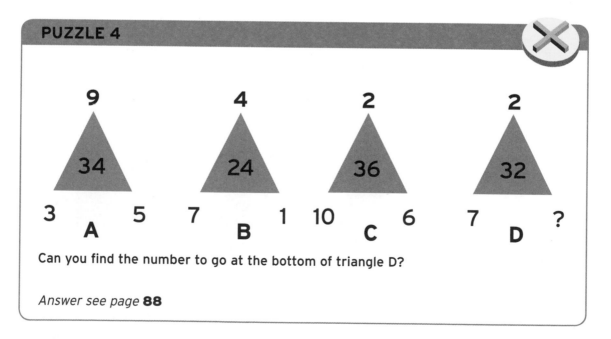

Can you find the number to go at the bottom of triangle D?

*Answer see page **88***

PUZZLE 5

This diagram was constructed according to a certain logic. Can you work out what number should replace the question mark?

Answer see page **88**

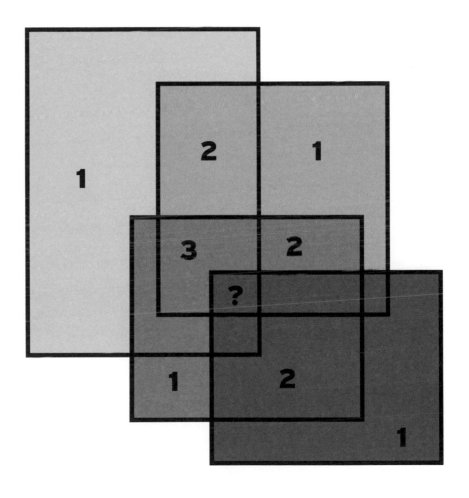

These tiles, when placed in the right order, will form a square in which
the first horizontal line is identical with the first vertical line and so on.
Can you successfully form the square?

Answer see page **88**

PUZZLE 7

Can you work out how the numbers in the triangles are related and find the missing number?

Answer see page **88**

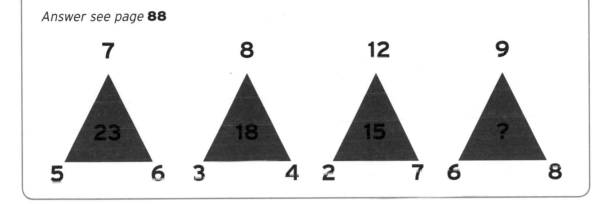

PUZZLE 8

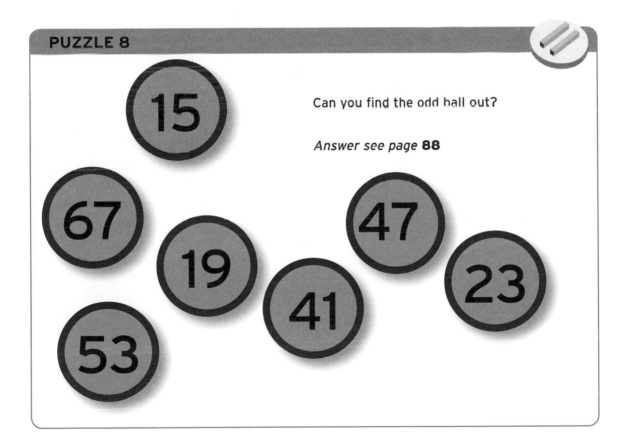

Can you find the odd ball out?

Answer see page **88**

1

2

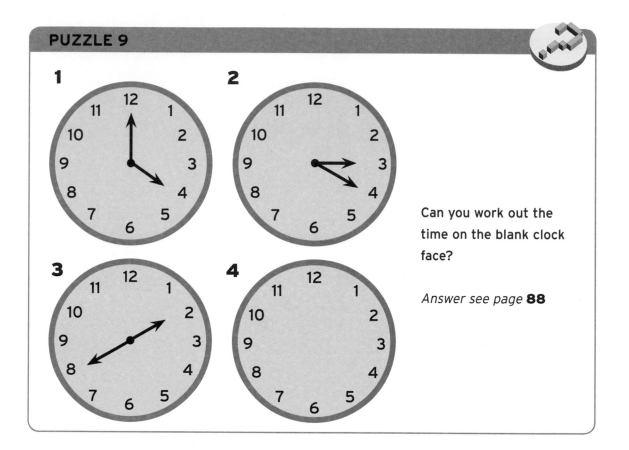

Can you work out the time on the blank clock face?

Answer see page 88

3

4

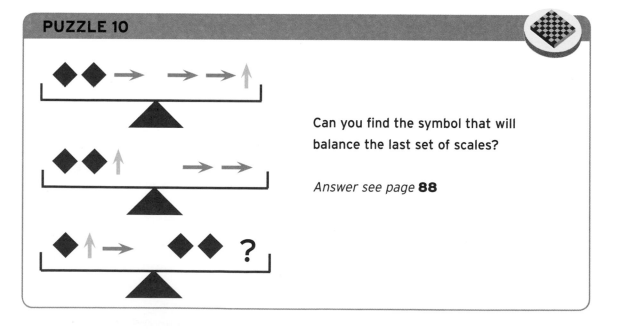

Can you find the symbol that will balance the last set of scales?

Answer see page 88

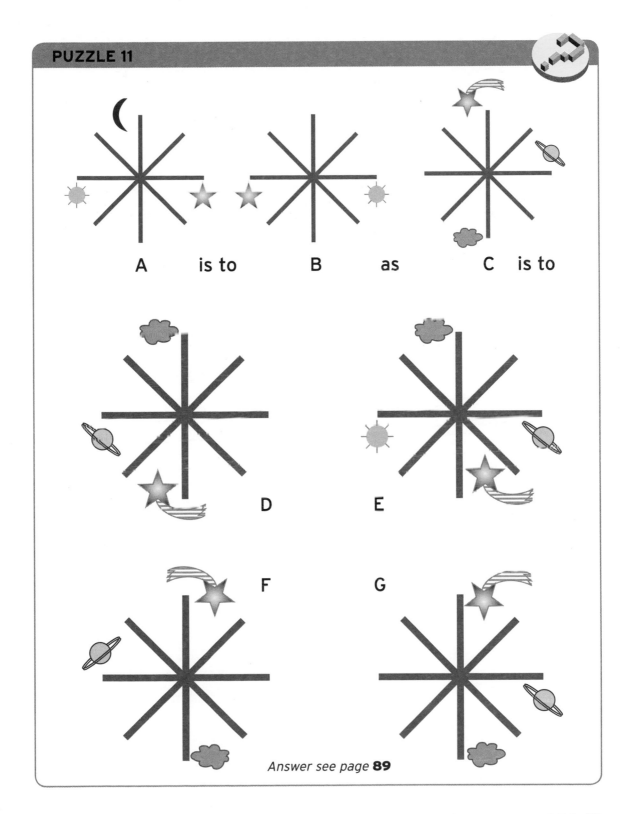

A   is to   B   as   C is to

D   E

F   G

Answer see page **89**

PUZZLE 12

Can you find the odd face out?

Answer see page **89**

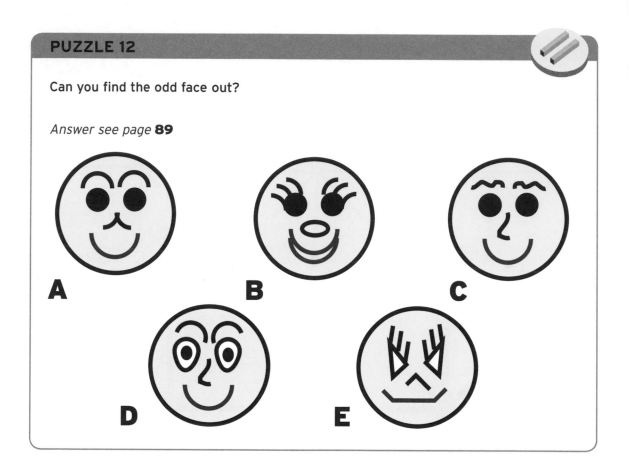

PUZZLE 13

Find the missing number.

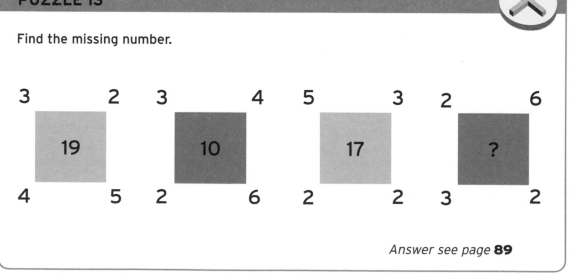

Answer see page **89**

PUZZLE 14

Which matchstick man, G, H or I, would carry on the sequence?

Answer see page **89**

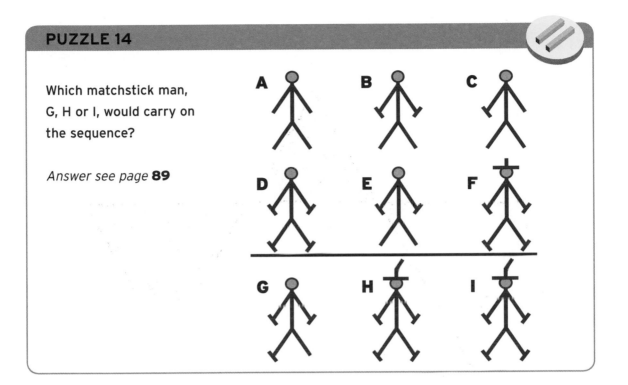

PUZZLE 15

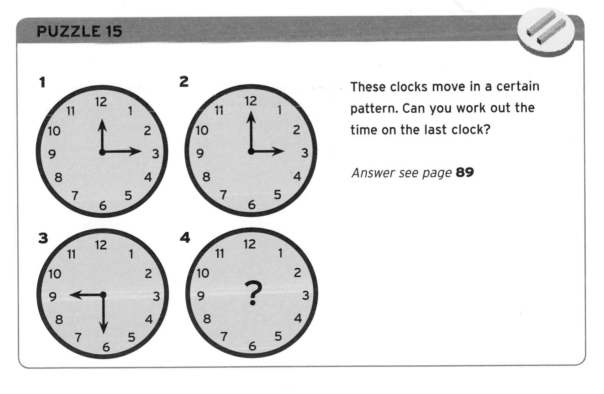

These clocks move in a certain pattern. Can you work out the time on the last clock?

Answer see page **89**

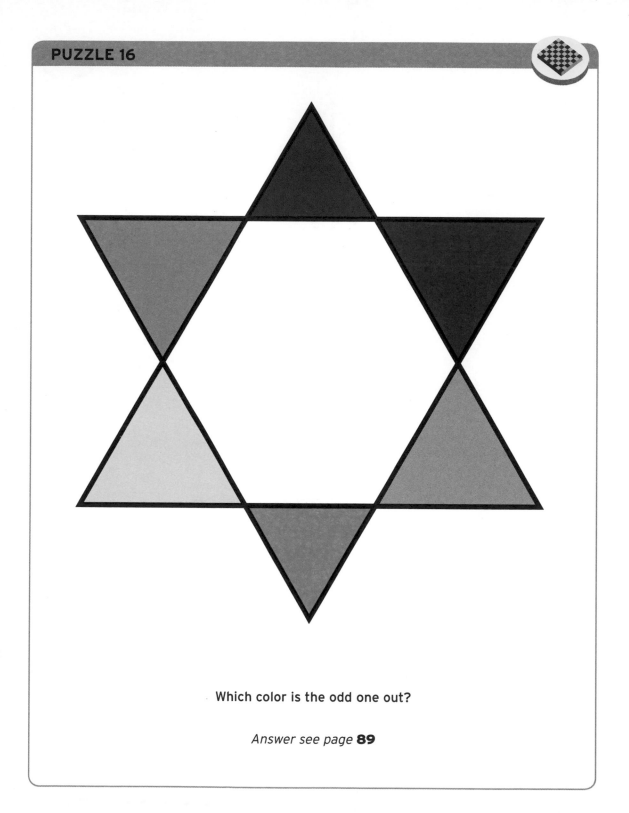

Which color is the odd one out?

Answer see page **89**

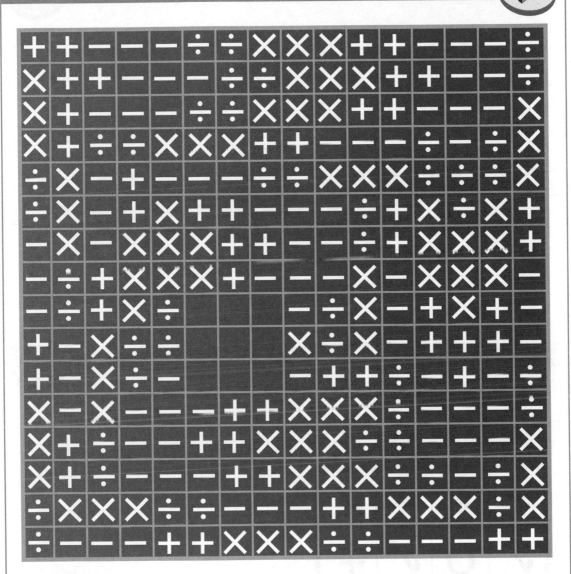

The symbols in the above grid follow a pattern. Can you work it out and find the missing section so that the logic of the grid is restored?

Answer see page **89**

PUZZLE 18

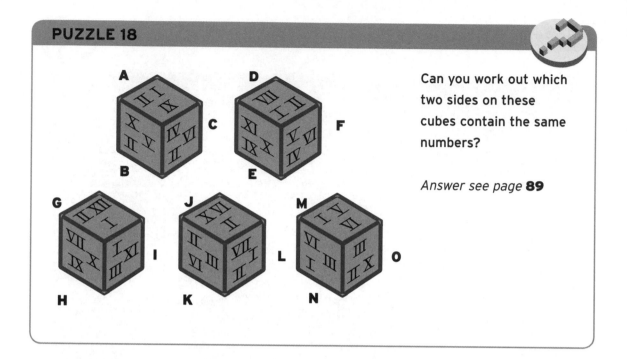

Can you work out which two sides on these cubes contain the same numbers?

Answer see page **89**

PUZZLE 19

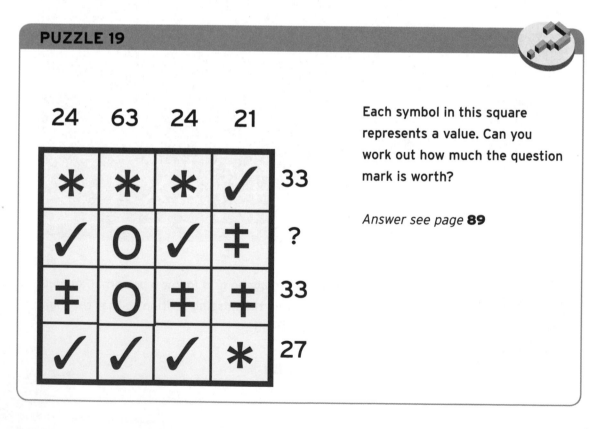

24   63   24   21

Each symbol in this square represents a value. Can you work out how much the question mark is worth?

Answer see page **89**

Two sides of these cubes contain the same
letters. Can you spot them?

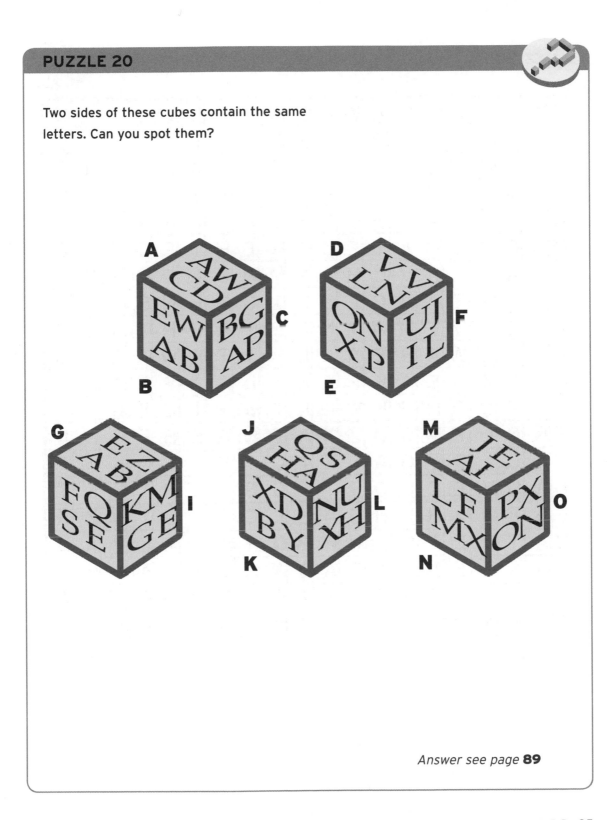

*Answer see page **89***

```
C W C O A L M K W O E A C K L G O Z A N
L H E M I N G W A Y N E I Y L M O X A E
L E E C M O X K W A X F E X A N B K O S
C F A K K E N Z A E X L A E B L P E F B
A Y E L H M Z N O E X I A I F H R K L I
M O Q V T O A T E U I W E H T E O G M O
A T K V L A V C H A E M N O L E U A B C
F S I A T A M Q L S D I C K E N S S T A
A L S T V E M W M N O E I A C H T A C T
F O O X W A B E A L L E I T A W W A C G
G T O X A E A K F A K I L A A S T A W N
O N F B C H J K W L L T J I I E X G H I
E N O L F M G O Z X A Y N A E B E C W L
R V O L F I G A E Z I U I E J C C K T P
E W U V E C U O P T E G B P N H T S E I
C S E W X H L H J A L E C E K L T U Z K
U A T A E E C K U W P Q R A R A E P A Z
A U S T E N X A T A Q W A L E T A W V E
H A P E X E A B C B A C A E W W E X L E
C C W A O R W E L L K M N O P P E L T U
```

Austen	Hemingway	Michener
Chaucer	Huxley	Orwell
Chekhov	Ibsen	Proust
Dickens	Kafka	Tolstoy
Flaubert	Kipling	Twain
Goethe	Lawrence	Zola

In this grid are hidden the names of 18 famous authors. Can you detect them? You can go forward or in reverse, in horizontal, vertical and diagonal lines.

Answer see page 89

PUZZLE 22

These tiles, when placed in the right order, will form a square in which the first horizontal line is identical with the first vertical line, and so on. Can you successfully form the square?

Answer see page **90**

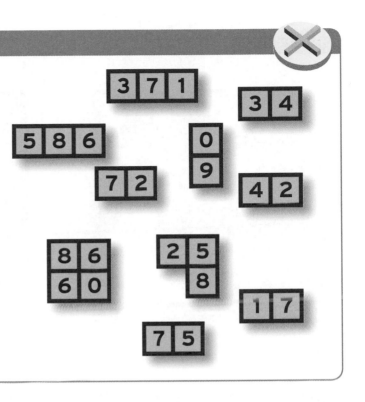

PUZZLE 23

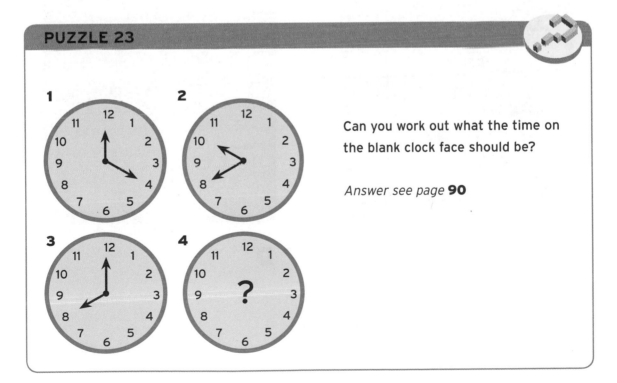

1

2

3

4

Can you work out what the time on the blank clock face should be?

Answer see page **90**

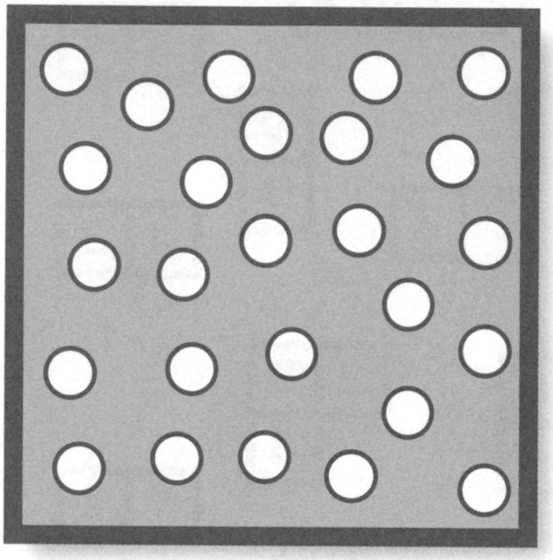

A

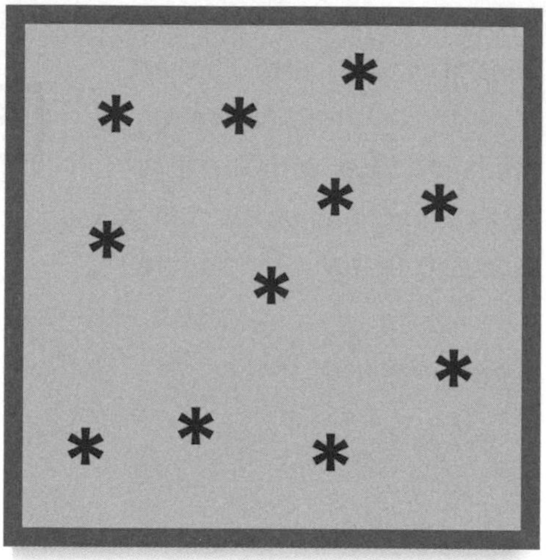

B

C

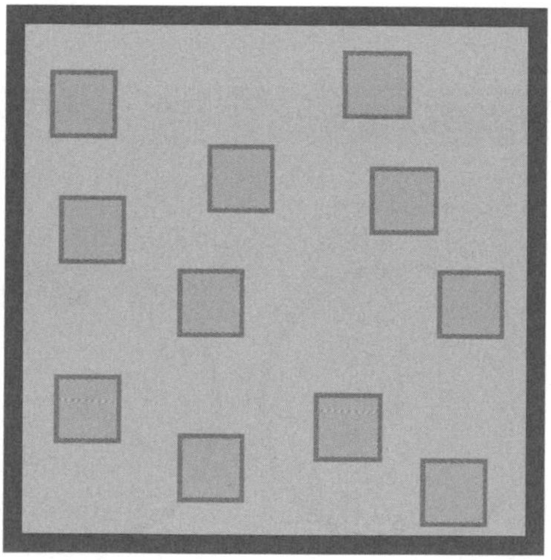

D

There is a logic to the patterns in these squares but one does not fit. Can you find the odd one out?

Answer see page **90**

30   50   42   38

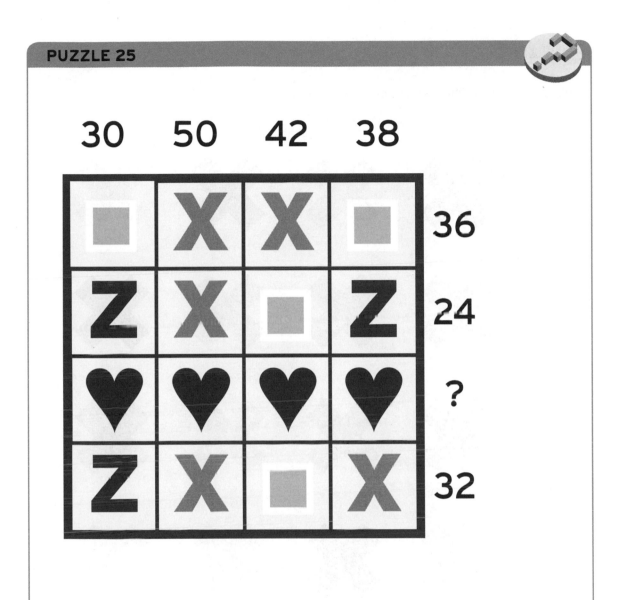

36

24

?

32

Each symbol in the square above represents a number. Can you find out how much the question mark is worth?

Answer see page **90**

Which of these is the odd one out?

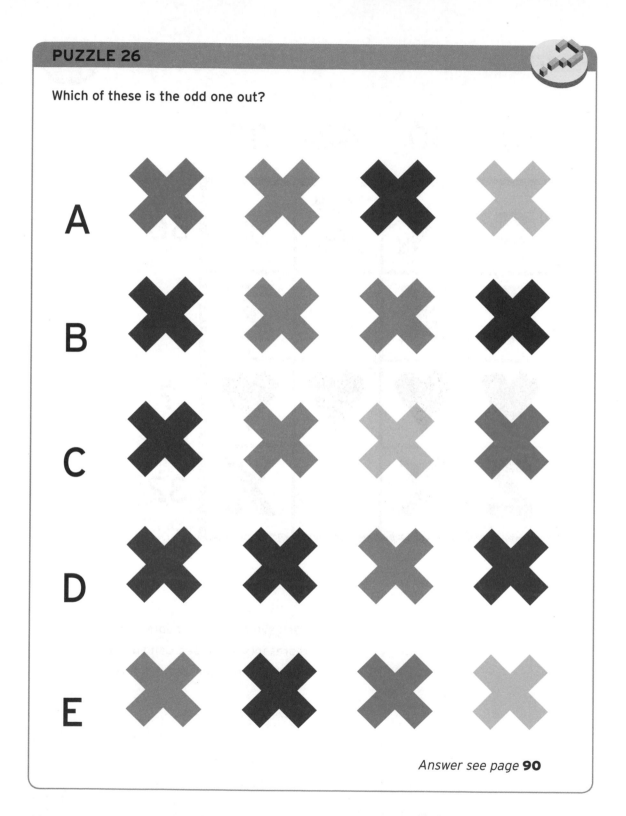

Answer see page **90**

PUZZLE 27

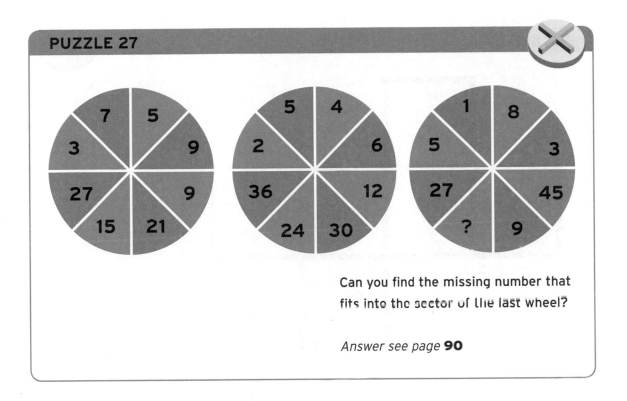

Can you find the missing number that fits into the sector of the last wheel?

Answer see page **90**

PUZZLE 28

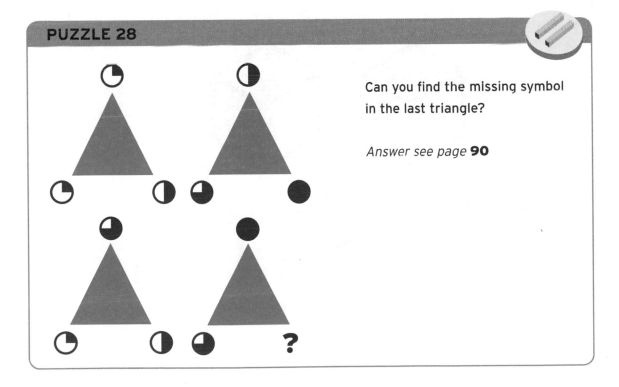

Can you find the missing symbol in the last triangle?

Answer see page **90**

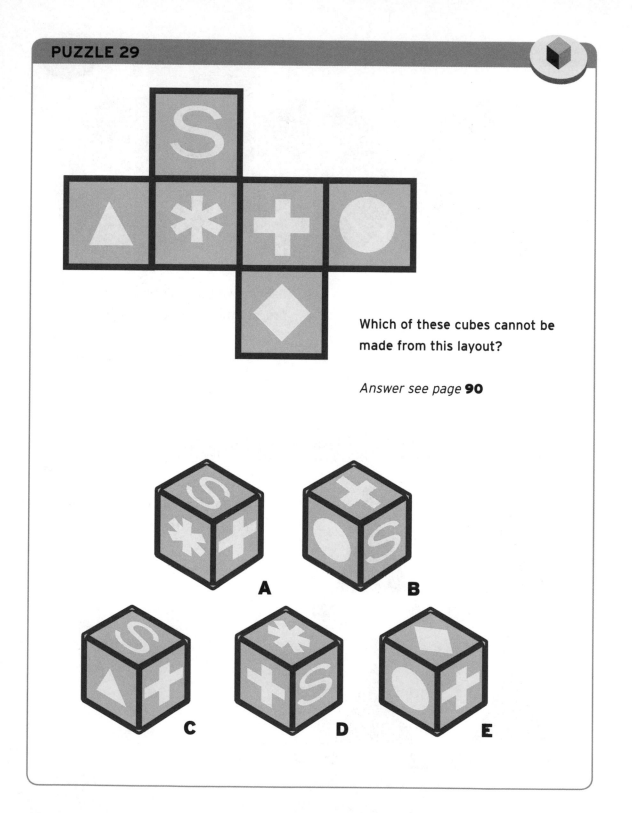

Which of these cubes cannot be made from this layout?

Answer see page **90**

PUZZLE 30

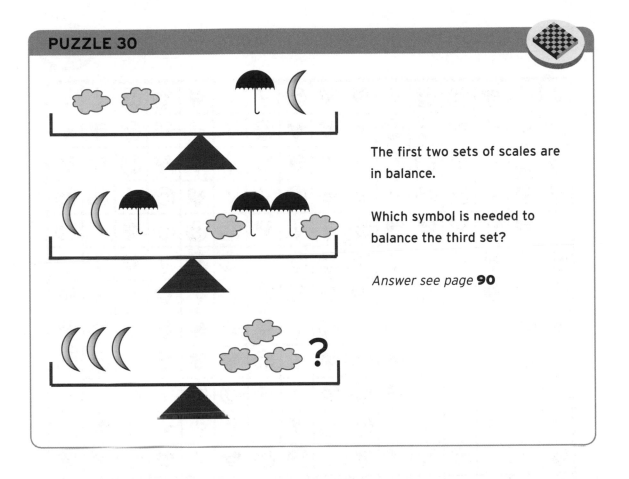

The first two sets of scales are in balance.

Which symbol is needed to balance the third set?

Answer see page **90**

PUZZLE 31

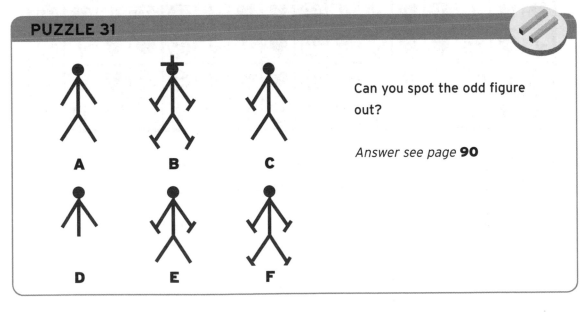

Can you spot the odd figure out?

Answer see page **90**

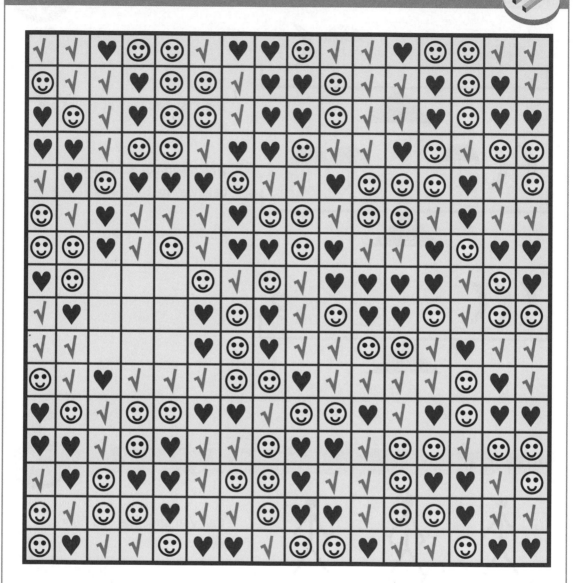

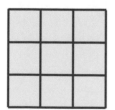

The symbols in the above grid follow a pattern. Can you work it out and find the missing section?

Answer see page **90**

PUZZLE 33

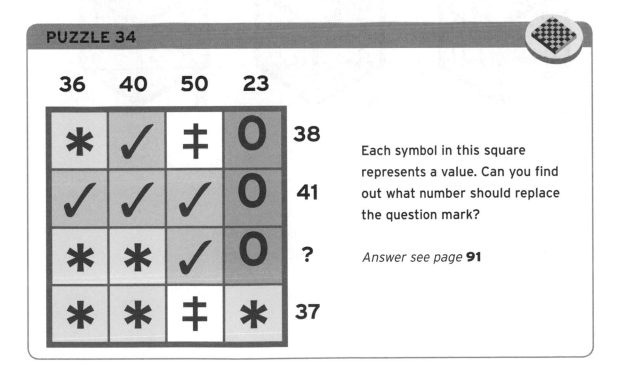

Can you work out what mathematical signs should replace the question marks so that both sections of the diagram arrive at the same value greater than 1. You have a choice between ÷ or x.

Answer see page **91**

PUZZLE 34

36	40	50	23	
✳	✓	‡	0	38
✓	✓	✓	0	41
✳	✳	✓	0	?
✳	✳	‡	✳	37

Each symbol in this square represents a value. Can you find out what number should replace the question mark?

Answer see page **91**

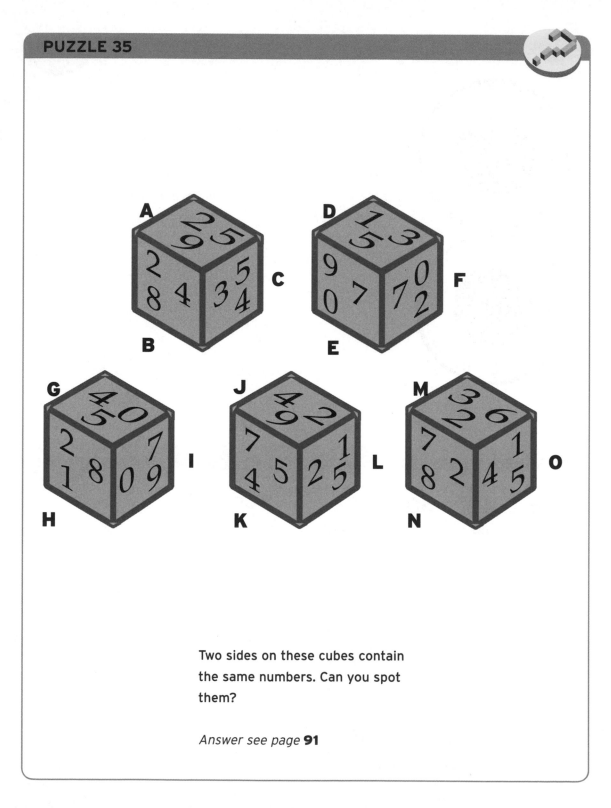

Two sides on these cubes contain the same numbers. Can you spot them?

Answer see page **91**

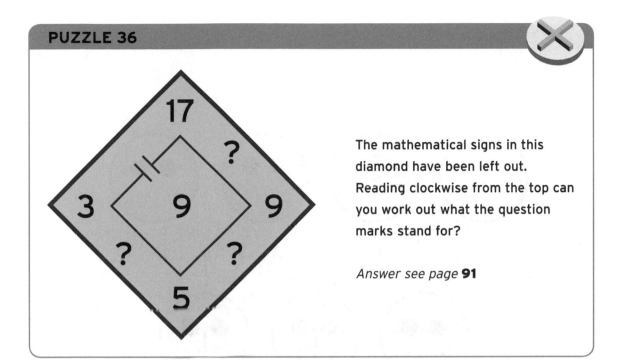

The mathematical signs in this diamond have been left out. Reading clockwise from the top can you work out what the question marks stand for?

Answer see page **91**

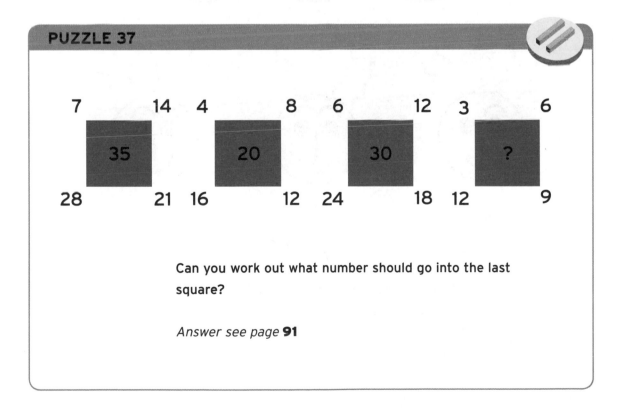

Can you work out what number should go into the last square?

Answer see page **91**

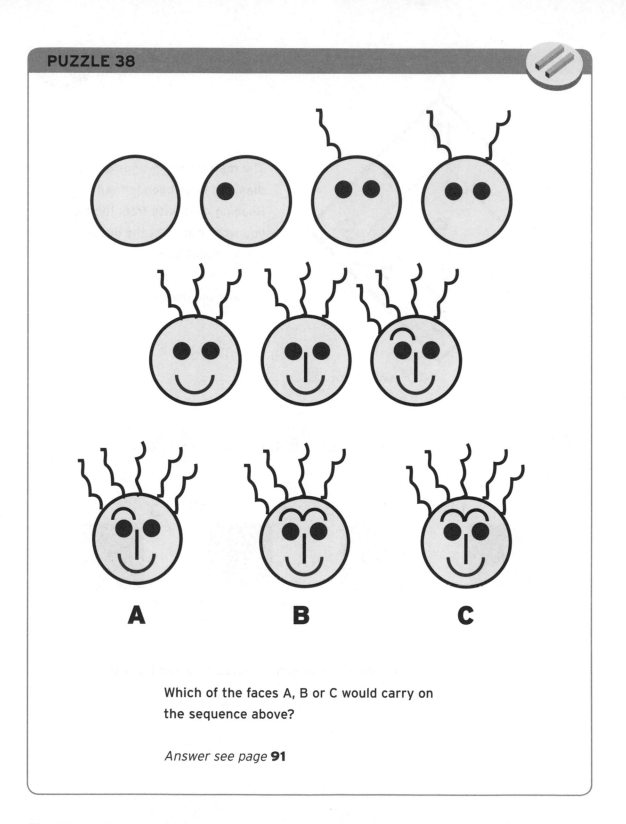

Which of the faces A, B or C would carry on
the sequence above?

Answer see page **91**

PUZZLE 39

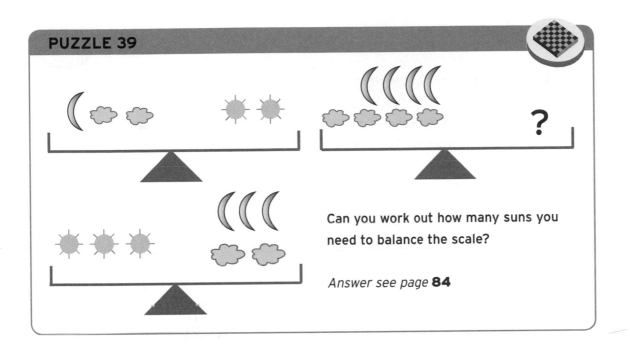

Can you work out how many suns you need to balance the scale?

Answer see page **84**

PUZZLE 40

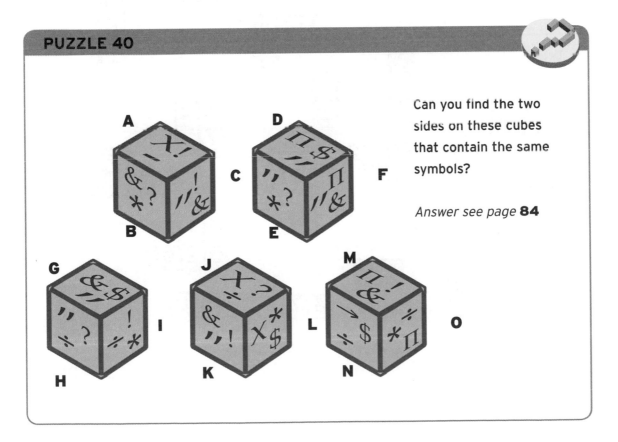

Can you find the two sides on these cubes that contain the same symbols?

Answer see page **84**

These tiles when placed in the right order will form a square in which the first horizontal line is identical with the first vertical line, and so on. Can you successfully form the square?

*Answer see page **91***

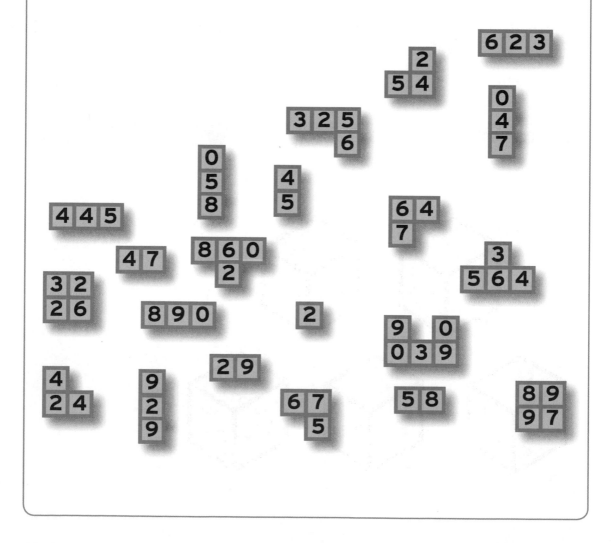

PUZZLE 42

36   23   24   ?

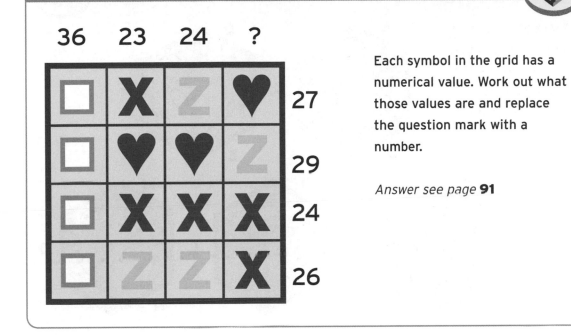

27
29
24
26

Each symbol in the grid has a numerical value. Work out what those values are and replace the question mark with a number.

Answer see page **91**

PUZZLE 43

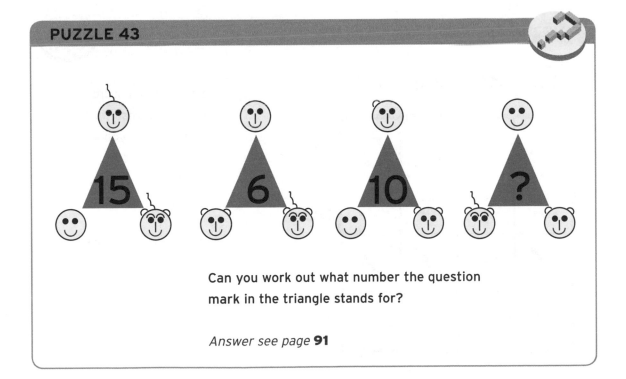

Can you work out what number the question mark in the triangle stands for?

Answer see page **91**

PUZZLE 44

There are two sides on these cubes that contain exactly the same symbols. Can you spot them?

Answer see page **91**

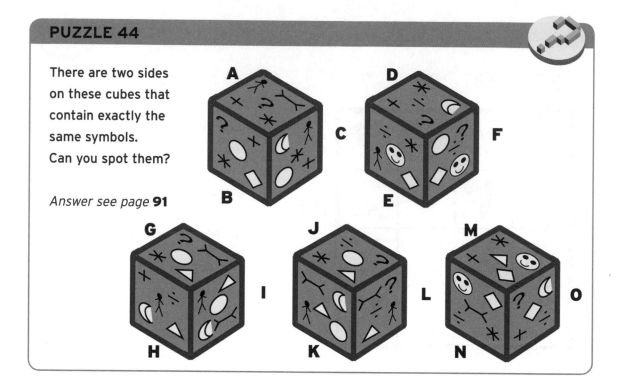

PUZZLE 45

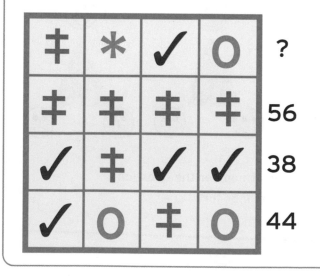

Each symbol in this square represents a number. Can you work out what number should replace the question mark?

Answer see page **91**

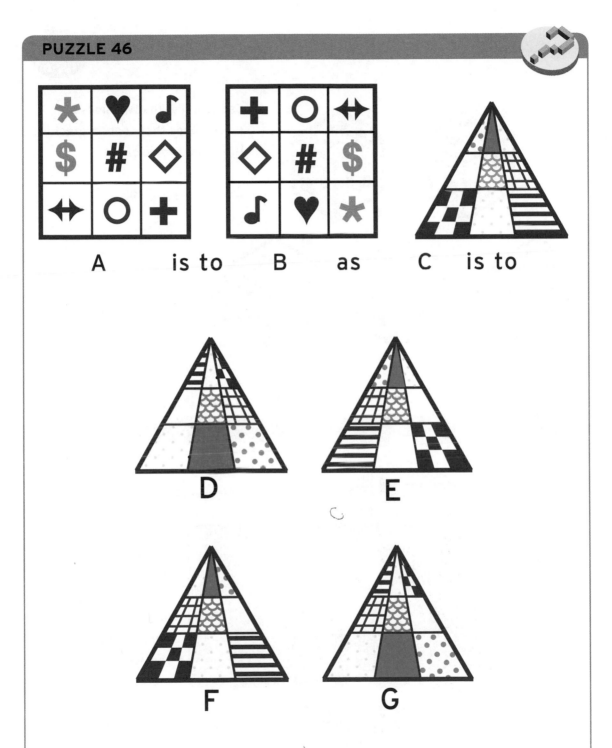

A is to B as C is to

D

E

F

G

Answer see page **91**

PUZZLE 47

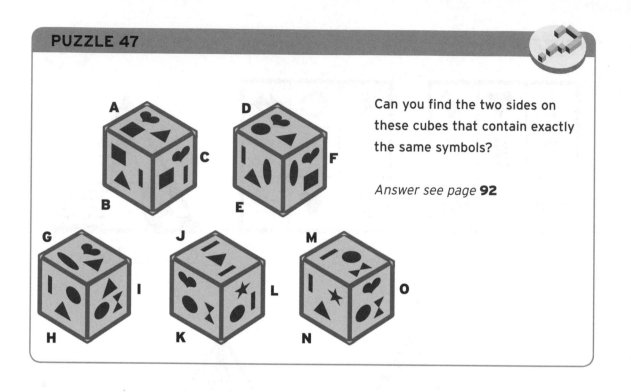

Can you find the two sides on these cubes that contain exactly the same symbols?

Answer see page **92**

PUZZLE 48

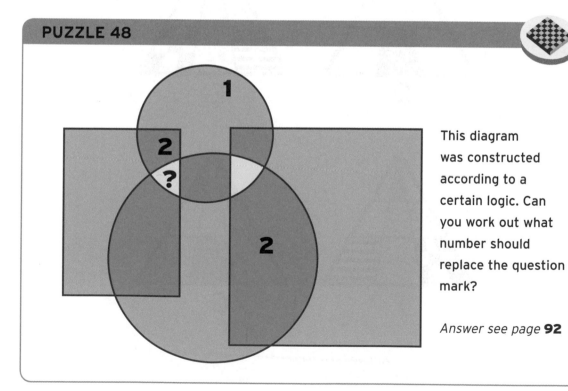

This diagram was constructed according to a certain logic. Can you work out what number should replace the question mark?

Answer see page **92**

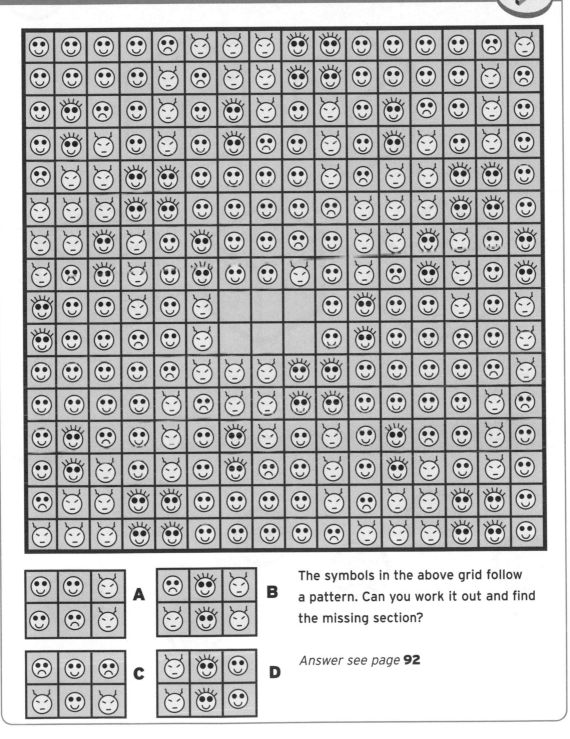

The symbols in the above grid follow a pattern. Can you work it out and find the missing section?

Answer see page 92

PUZZLE 50

Can you work out which two sides on these cubes contain the same symbols?

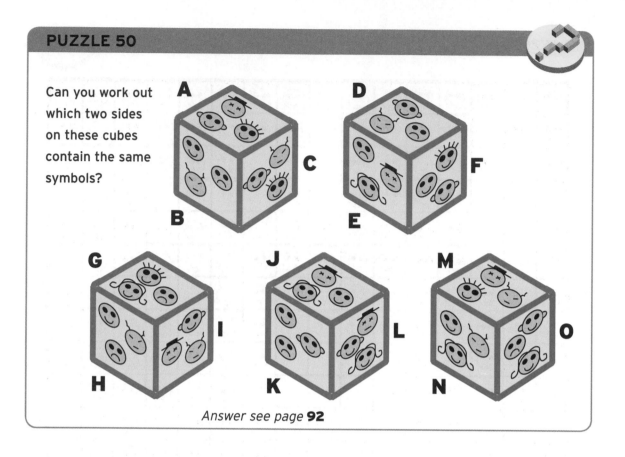

Answer see page **92**

PUZZLE 51

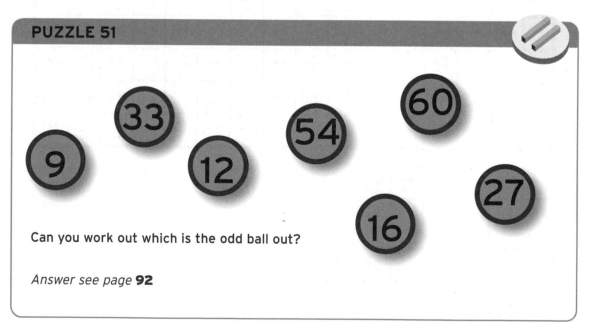

Can you work out which is the odd ball out?

Answer see page **92**

PUZZLE 52

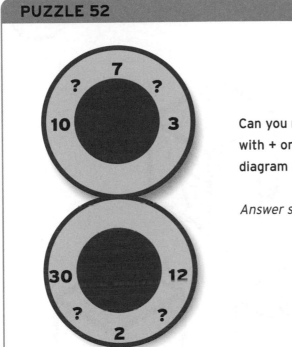

Can you replace the question marks with + or - so that both sections in this diagram add up to the same value?

Answer see page **92**

PUZZLE 53

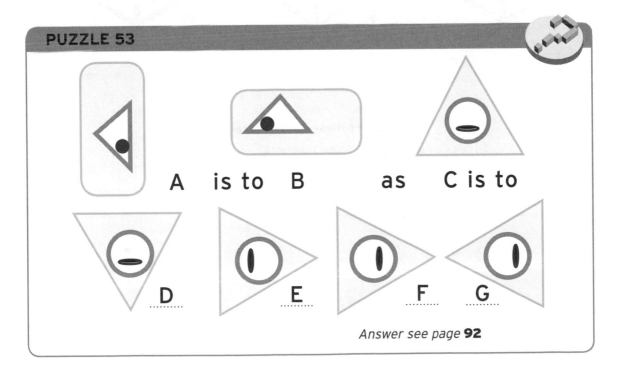

A   is to   B   as   C is to

D   E   F   G

Answer see page **92**

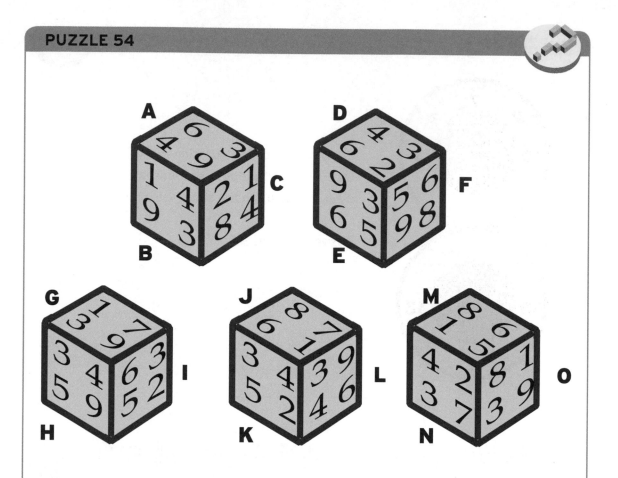

Two sides of these cubes contain
exactly the same numbers.
Can you spot them?

Answer see page **92**

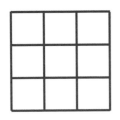

The symbols in this grid follow a pattern. Can you work it out and complete the missing section?

*Answer see page **92***

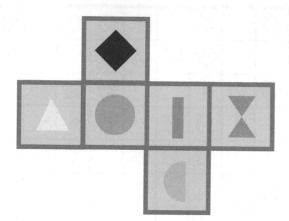

Which of these cubes cannot be made from this layout?

Answer see page **92**

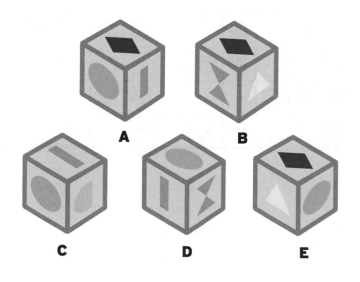

A

B

C

D

E

PUZZLE 57

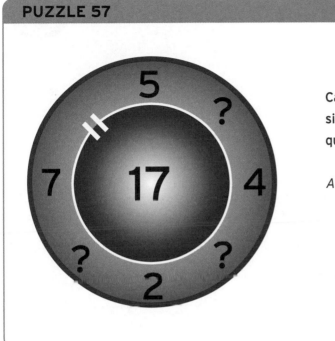

Can you find the mathematical signs that should replace the question marks in this diagram?

Answer see page **92**

PUZZLE 58

The four triangles are linked by a simple mathematical formula. Can you discover what it is and then find the odd one out?

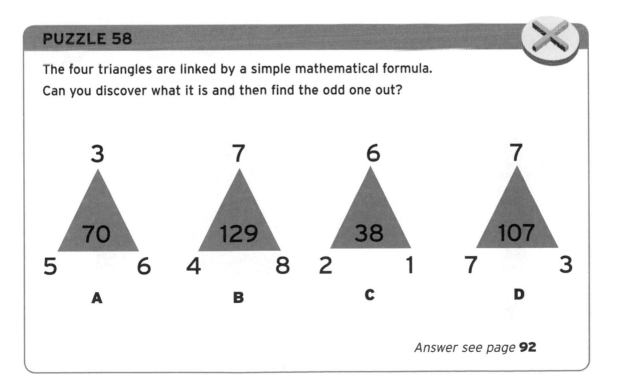

Answer see page **92**

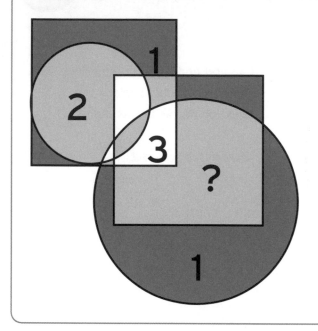

Can you crack the logic of
this diagram and replace the
question mark
with a number?

Answer see page **92**

How would you continue this series?

Answer see page **92**

PUZZLE 61

These tiles when placed in the right order will form a square in which the first horizontal line is identical with the first vertical line, and so. Can you successfully form the square?

Answer see page **93**

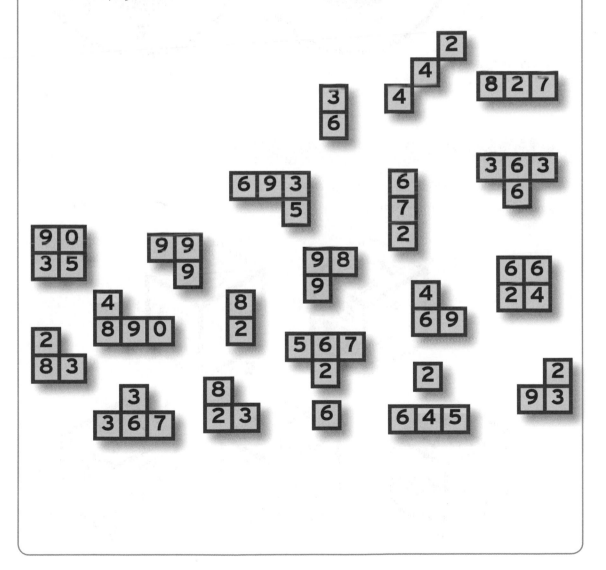

PUZZLE 62

Can you replace the question marks in this diagram with the symbols x and ÷ so that both sections arrive at the same value?

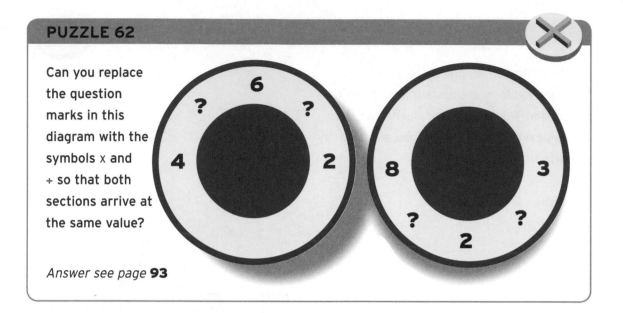

Answer see page **93**

PUZZLE 63

Can you work out which three sides of these cubes contain the same symbols?

Answer see page **93**

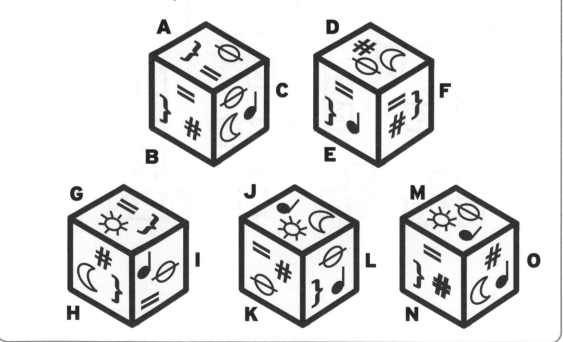

PUZZLE 64

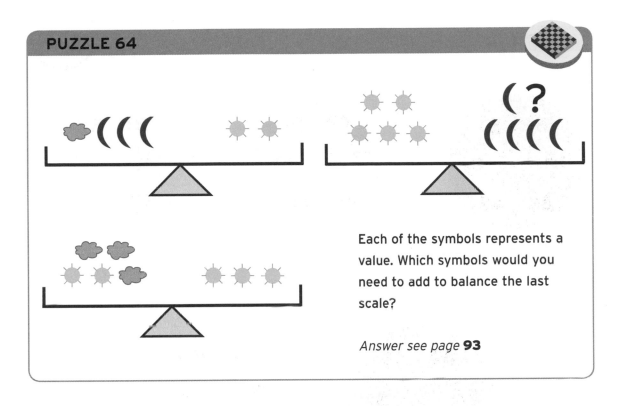

Each of the symbols represents a value. Which symbols would you need to add to balance the last scale?

*Answer see page **93***

PUZZLE 65

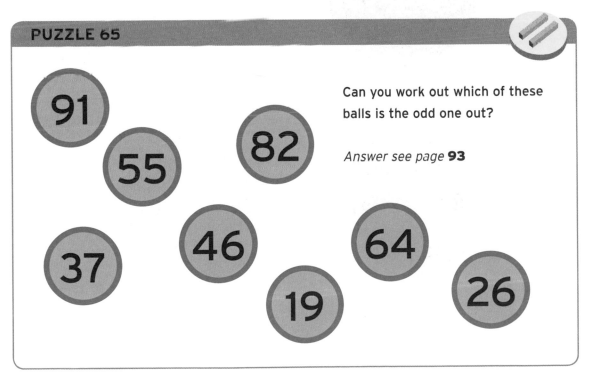

Can you work out which of these balls is the odd one out?

*Answer see page **93***

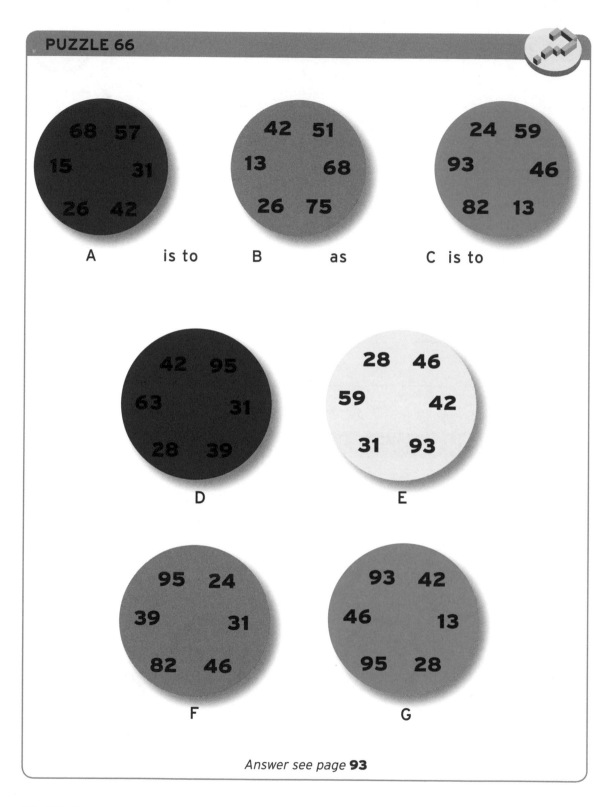

A is to B as C is to

D

E

F

G

*Answer see page **93***

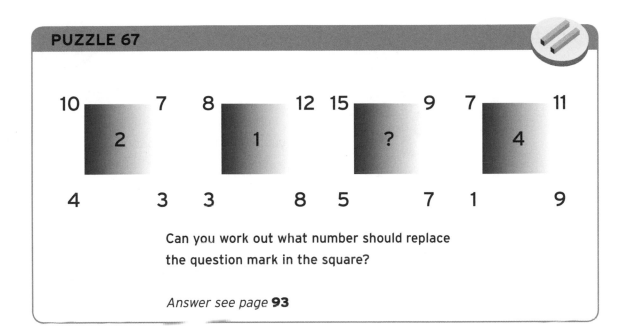

10   7   8   12   15   9   7   11
  2   1   ?   4
4   3   3   8   5   7   1   9

Can you work out what number should replace
the question mark in the square?

Answer see page **93**

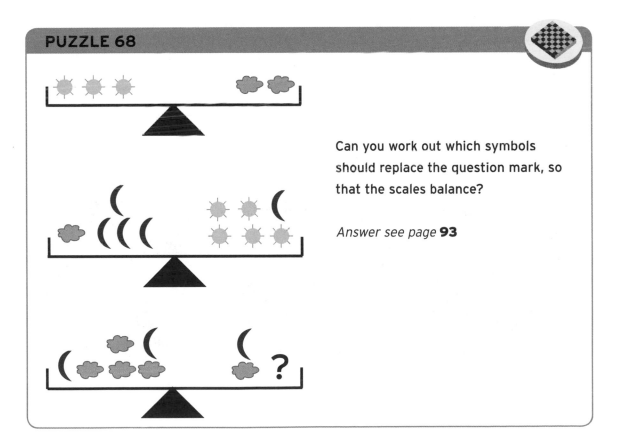

Can you work out which symbols
should replace the question mark, so
that the scales balance?

Answer see page **93**

PUZZLE 69

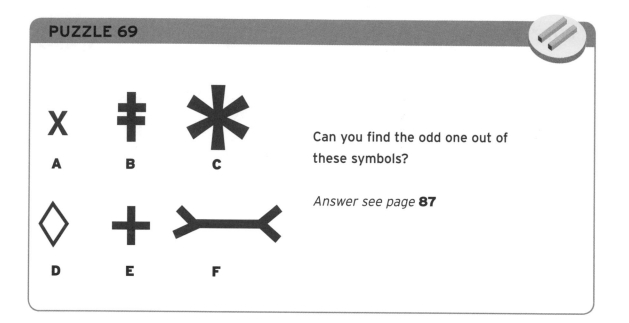

Can you find the odd one out of these symbols?

Answer see page **87**

PUZZLE 70

Can you work out what number should replace the question mark to follow the rules of the other wheels?

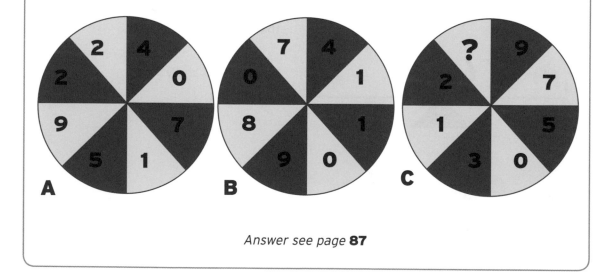

Answer see page **87**

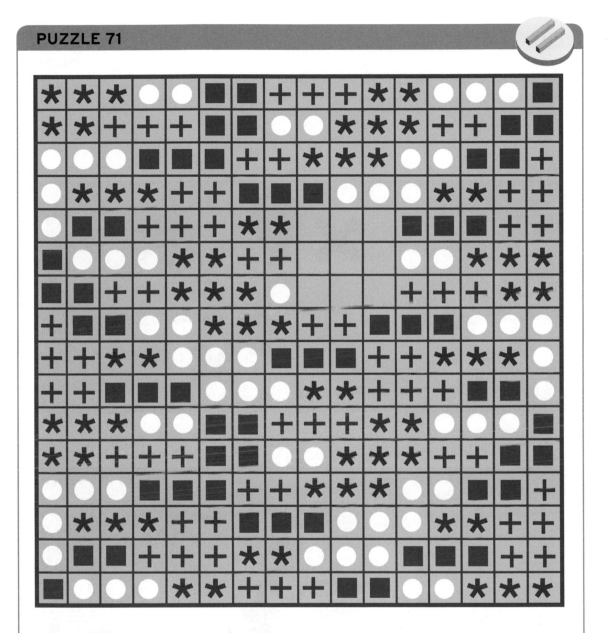

The symbols in this grid behave in a predictable manner. When you have discovered their sequence it should be possible to fill in the blank segment.

Answer see page 93

The two pictures are very similar but not quite identical.

Find 11 ways in which A differs from B.

A

B

Answer see page **94**

PUZZLE 73

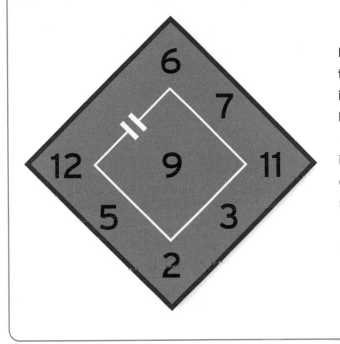

In this diagram, starting from the top of the diamond and working in a clockwise direction, the four basic mathematical signs (+, -, x, ÷) have been omitted. Your task is to restore them so that the calculation, with the answer in the middle, is correct.

Answer see page **94**

PUZZLE 74

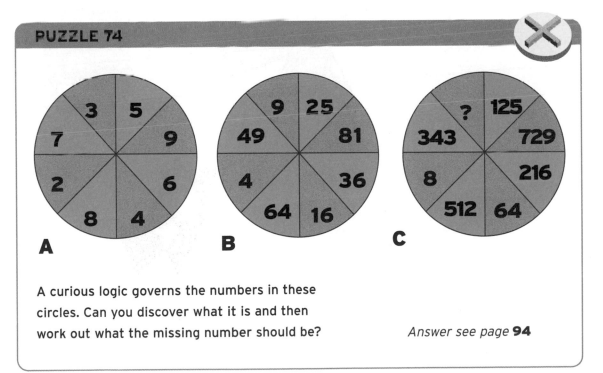

A curious logic governs the numbers in these circles. Can you discover what it is and then work out what the missing number should be?

Answer see page **94**

PUZZLE 75

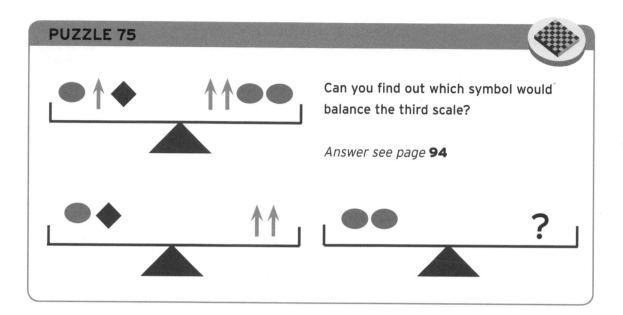

Can you find out which symbol would balance the third scale?

Answer see page **94**

PUZZLE 76

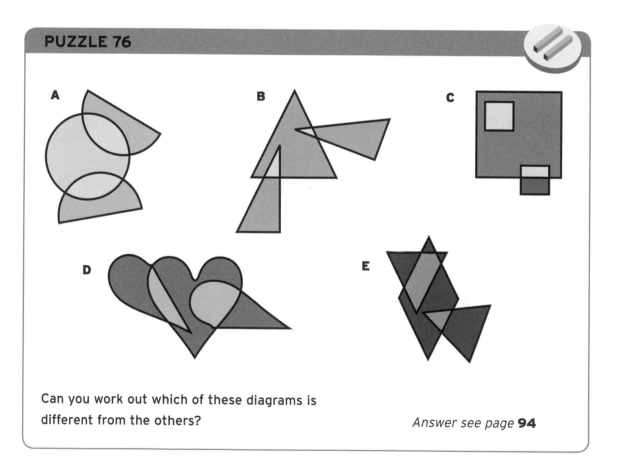

A

B

C

D

E

Can you work out which of these diagrams is different from the others?

Answer see page **94**

PUZZLE 77

Can you work out what the blank clockface should look like?

Answer see page **94**

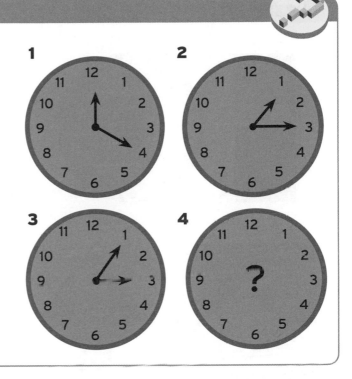

PUZZLE 78

35	47	38	24	
‡	✳	✳	✳	?
✓	‡	‡	✓	40
✓	O	✓	✓	21
O	O	O	O	48

Can you work out what number each symbol represents and find the value of the question mark?

Answer see page **94**

PUZZLE 79

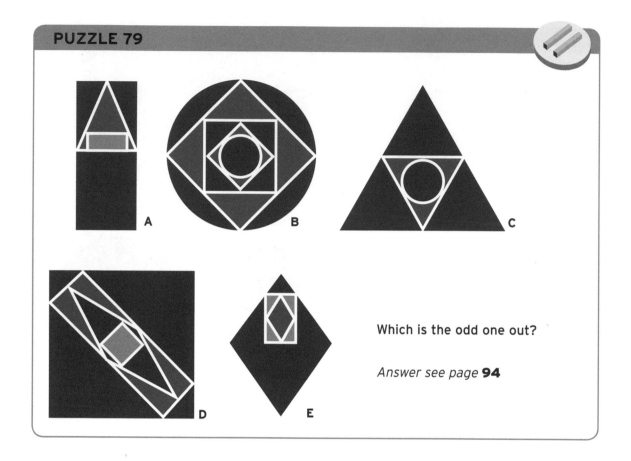

Which is the odd one out?

Answer see page **94**

PUZZLE 80

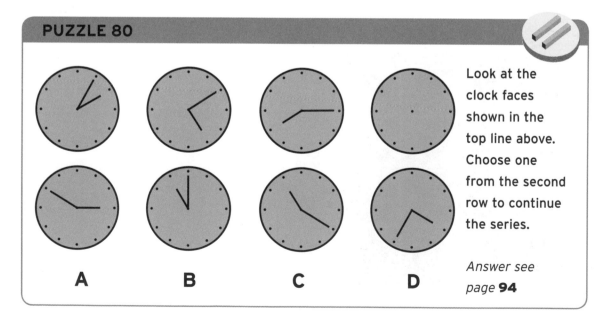

Look at the clock faces shown in the top line above. Choose one from the second row to continue the series.

Answer see page **94**

A   B   C   D

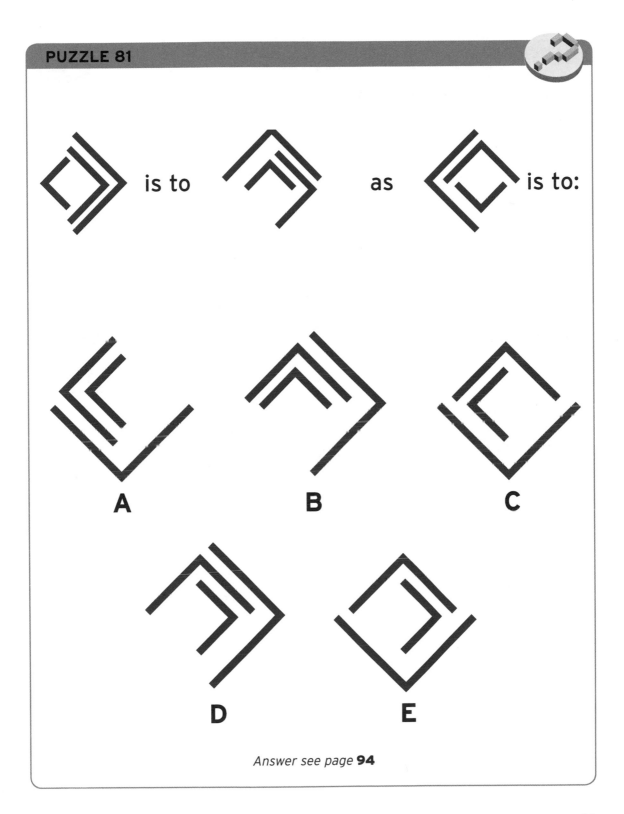

Answer see page **94**

PUZZLE 82

Which of the following shapes forms a perfect triangle when combined with the picture on the right?

*Answer see page **94***

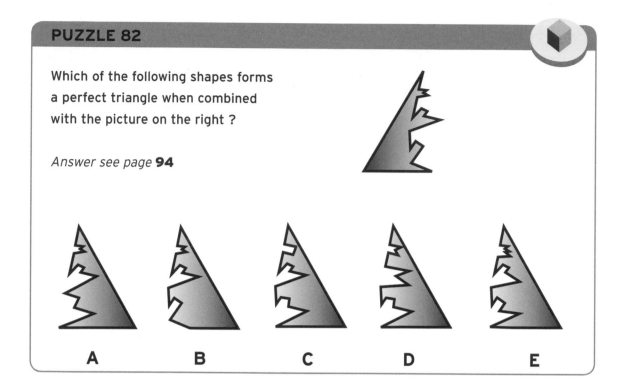

A   B   C   D   E

PUZZLE 83

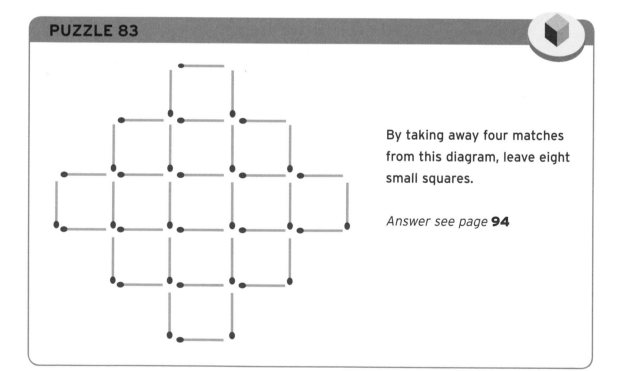

By taking away four matches from this diagram, leave eight small squares.

*Answer see page **94***

PUZZLE 84

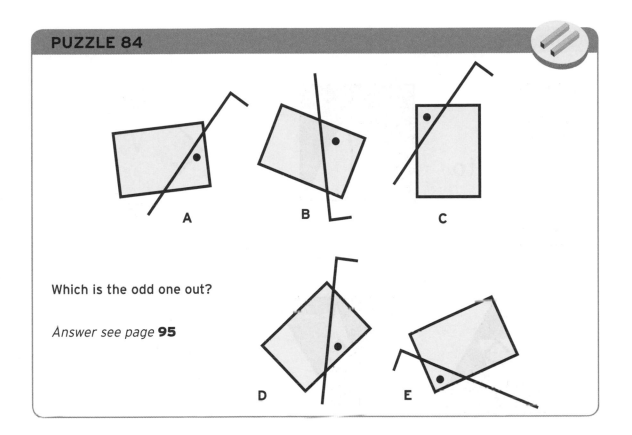

Which is the odd one out?

Answer see page **95**

PUZZLE 85

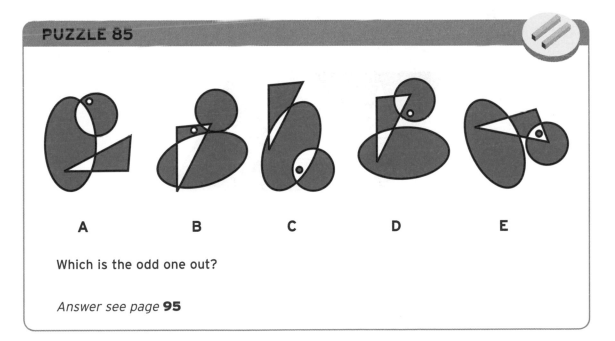

A   B   C   D   E

Which is the odd one out?

Answer see page **95**

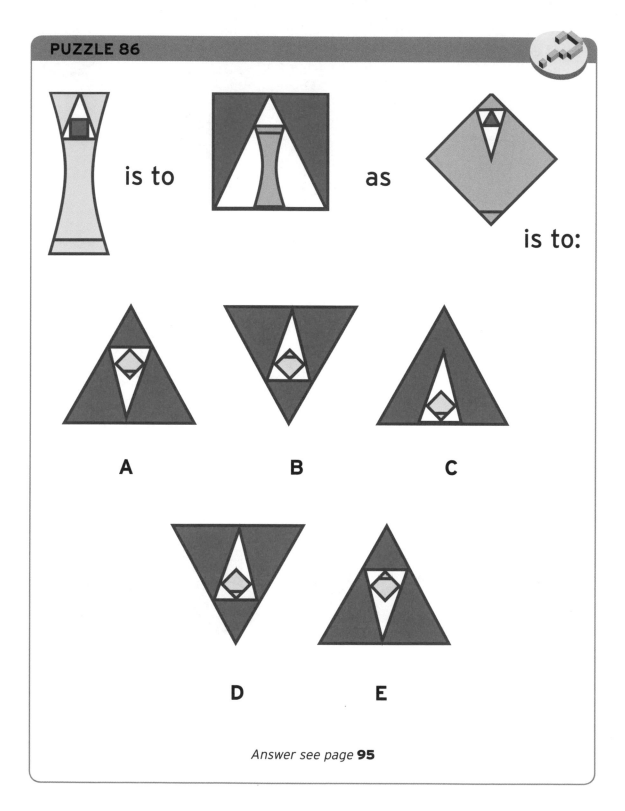

is to

as

is to:

A

B

C

D

E

Answer see page 95

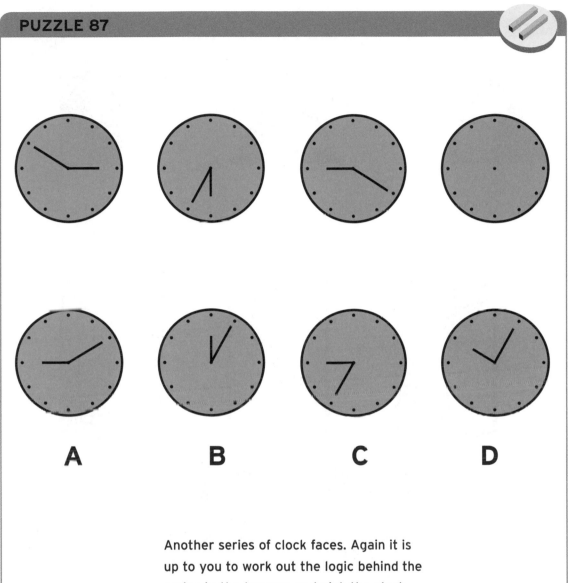

A   **B**   **C**   **D**

Another series of clock faces. Again it is up to you to work out the logic behind the series in the top row and pick the clock from the bottom row that replaces the blank clock.

Answer see page **95**

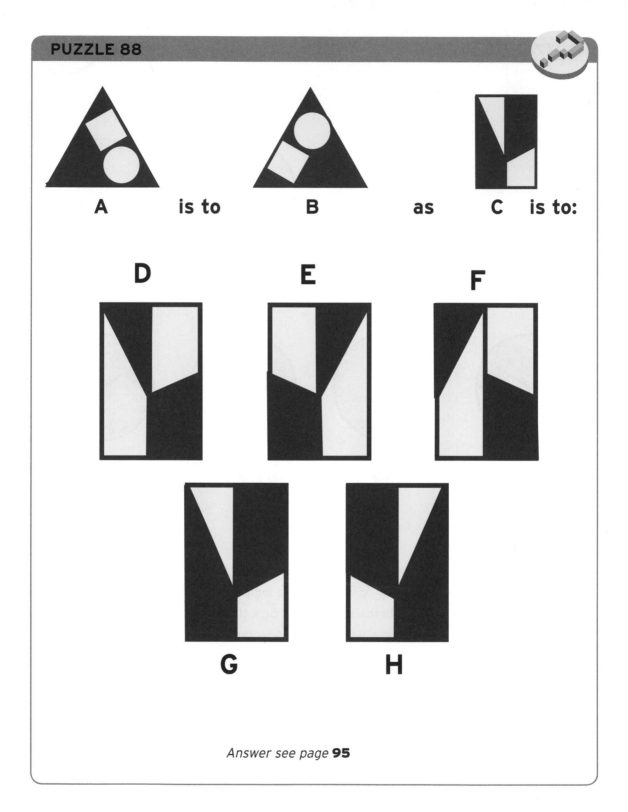

A   is to   B   as   C   is to:

D

E

F

G

H

Answer see page 95

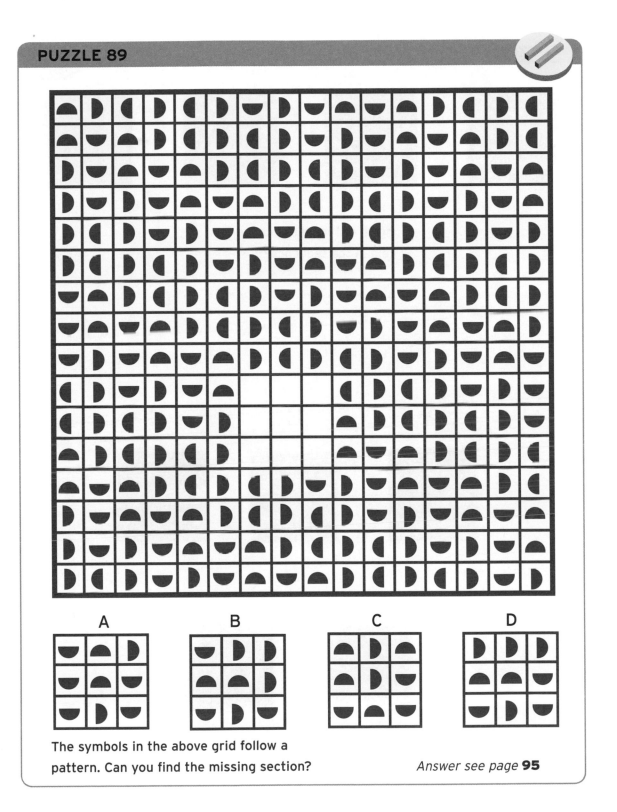

The symbols in the above grid follow a
pattern. Can you find the missing section?

Answer see page **95**

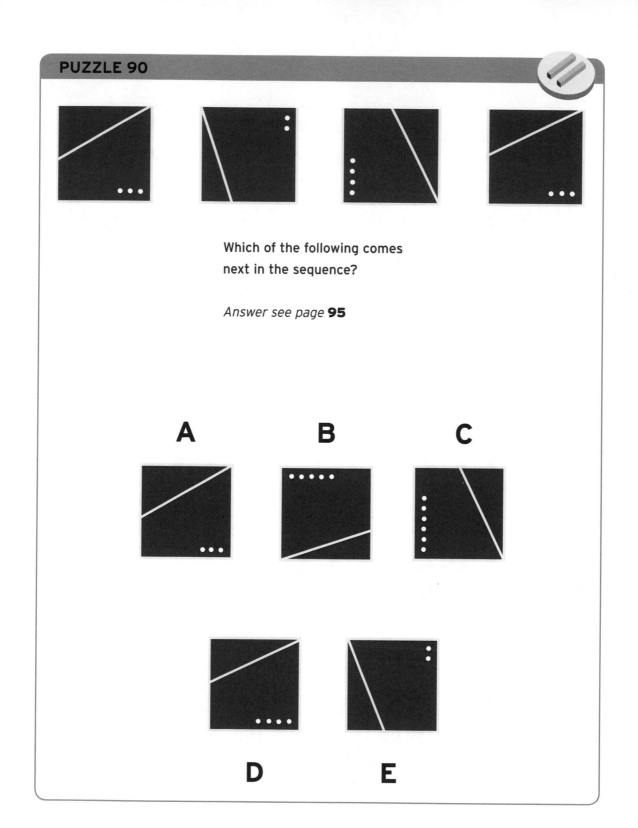

Which of the following comes
next in the sequence?

Answer see page **95**

A

B

C

D

E

PUZZLE 91

Can you work out which sides on these cubes contain the same letters?

Answer see page **95**

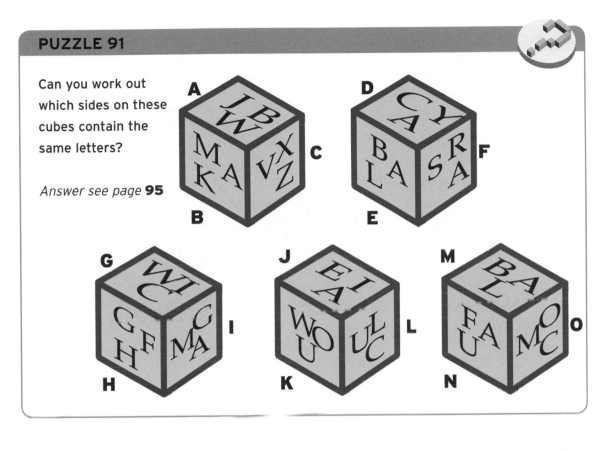

PUZZLE 92

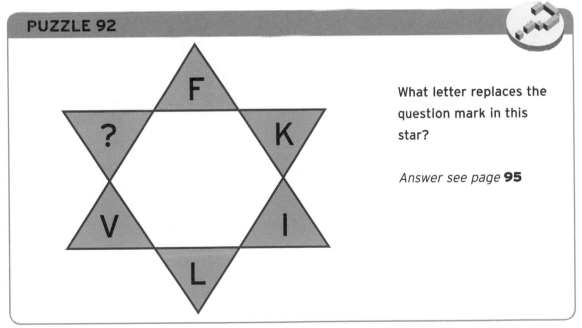

What letter replaces the question mark in this star?

Answer see page **95**

PUZZLE 93

In this diamond the mathematical signs +, -, x and ÷ have been left out. Can you work out which sign fits between each pair of numbers to arrive at the number in the middle of the diagram? To start you off, three of the signs are each used twice.

Answer see page **95**

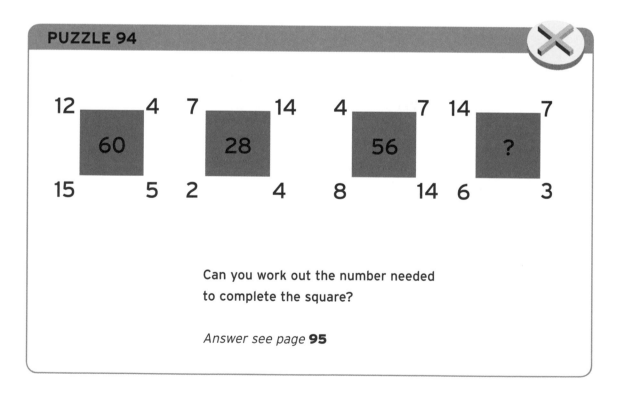

PUZZLE 94

12 — 4   7 — 14   4 — 7   14 — 7

60   28   56   ?

15   5   2   4   8   14   6   3

Can you work out the number needed to complete the square?

Answer see page **95**

Someone has made a mistake decorating this
cake. Can you correct the pattern?

Answer see page **95**

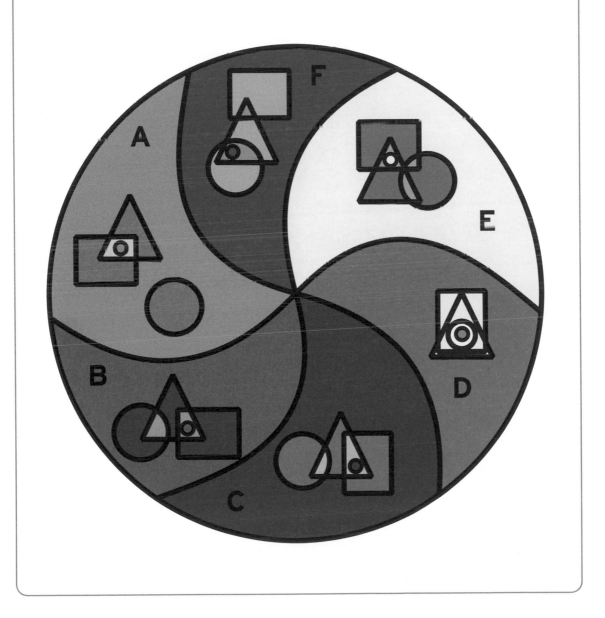

Easy Answers

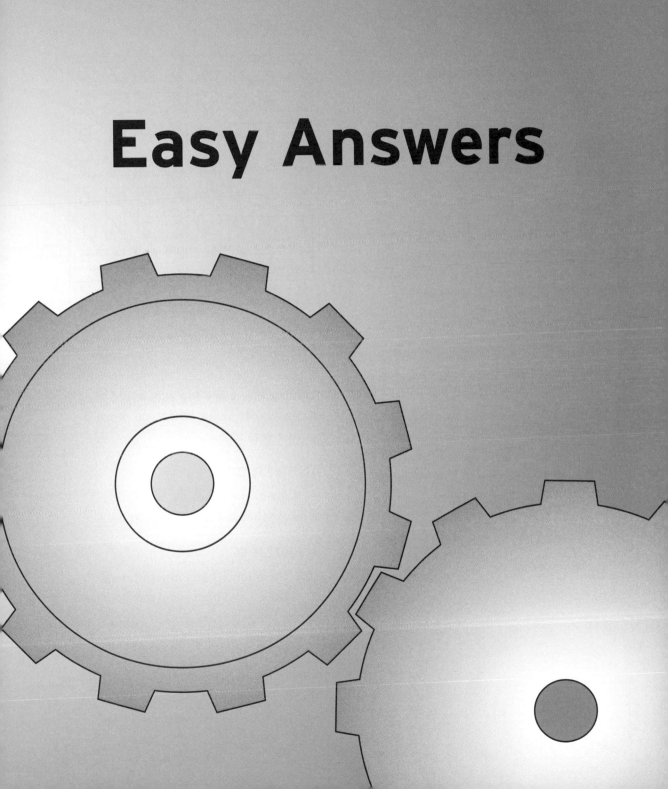

ANSWER 1

E. In all the others the colors follow the same sequence: light blue, red, dark blue, green, yellow, pink.

ANSWER 2

E.

ANSWER 3

4. Multiply the two numbers in the outer circle of each segment and place the product in the inner circle two segments away in a clockwise direction.

ANSWER 4

7. Add the three numbers at the corner of each triangle, multiply by 2, and place that number in the middle.

ANSWER 5

4. There are 4 boxes and the number relates to the number of boxes in which the number is enclosed.

ANSWER 6

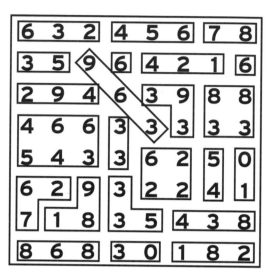

ANSWER 7

21. Add all the numbers of each triangle together and place the sum in the middle of the next triangle. When you reach D put the sum in A.

ANSWER 8

15. None of the other numbers have a divisor – they are all prime numbers.

ANSWER 9

1:00. The minute hand moves forward 20 minutes, the hour hand moves back 1 hour.

ANSWER 10

A diamond. (4 diamonds = 3 left/arrows = 6 up-arrows).

ANSWER 11

F. The symbols are reflected over a vertical line.

ANSWER 12

E. It contains no curved lines.

ANSWER 13

8. Add all the numbers together. In a yellow square you add 5 to the sum, in a green one you subtract 5.

ANSWER 14

G. Add 2 lines to the body, take away 1, add 3, take away 2, add 4, take away 3.

ANSWER 15

6:45. The minute hand moves back 15, 30 and 45 minutes. The hour hand moves forward 3, 6 and 9 hours.

ANSWER 16

Pink. All the other colors are either primary or secondary colors. Pink is a hue.

ANSWER 17

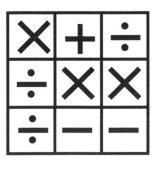

The order is 2 +, 3 -, 2 ÷, 3 x. The puzzle goes in an inward clockwise spiral starting from the top left corner.

ANSWER 18

D and L.

ANSWER 19

39. Tick = 6, star = 9, cross = 3, O = 24.

ANSWER 20

E and O. The letters are N, O, P and X.

ANSWER 21

Austen	Hemingway
Michener	Chaucer
Huxley	Orwell
Chekov	Ibsen
Proust	Dickens
Kafka	Tolstoy
Flaubert	Kipling
Twain	Goethe
Lawrence	Zola

ANSWER 22

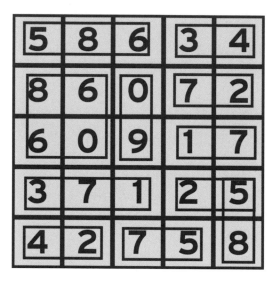

ANSWER 23

6:20. The minute hand advances 20 minutes each time, the hour hand goes back 2 hours each time.

ANSWER 24

B. The number of sides of the internal figures should increase by one each time. B is the odd one out because its internal figures should have 2 sides.

ANSWER 25

68. Square = 7; X = 11; Z = 3; Heart = 17.

ANSWER 26

C. In all other cases the first letters of the colors form words: gory, poor, prop, orgy.

ANSWER 27

72. Multiply all the numbers in the top sections to arrive at the number in the opposite bottom section. Multiply by 3 in the first circle, by 6 in the second one, and by 9 in the third circle.

ANSWER 28

A full circle. Go first along the top of the triangles, then along the bottoms. Each circle is filled one quarter at a time until the circle is complete, then reverts to one-quarter filled.

ANSWER 29

C.

ANSWER 30

One cloud. The values are: Cloud = 3; Umbrella = 2; Moon = 4.

ANSWER 31

C. It has an odd number of elements, the others all have an even number.

ANSWER 32

Start at the top right corner and work in a clockwise inward spiral. The pattern is:

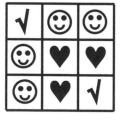 two ticks, one heart, two faces, one tick, two hearts, one face, etc.

ANSWER 33

Top half: ÷ x; bottom half: x x.

ANSWER 34

33. Star = 8; Tick = 12; Cross = 13; Circle = 5.

ANSWER 35

E and I.

ANSWER 36

- - x.

ANSWER 37

15. Start at the top left corner and add that number to each corner in a clockwise direction, eg. 7 + 7 = 14 + 7 = 21 + 7 = 28 + 7 = 35.

ANSWER 38

A. Add one new element to the face, then add one hair and an element to the face, then a hair, then a hair and an element to the face, repeat sequence.

ANSWER 39

Five suns. Moon = 2; Cloud = 3; Sun = 4.

ANSWER 40

C and K.

ANSWER 41

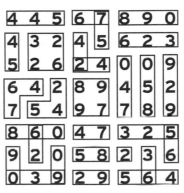

ANSWER 42

23. Square = 9; Cross = 5; Z = 6; Heart = 7.

ANSWER 43

2. The faces represent numbers, based on the elements in or around the face (excluding the head). Multiply the top number with the bottom right number and divide by the bottom left number. Place the answer in the middle.

ANSWER 44

I and K. The figures are: matchstick man, triangle, half-moon, circle, stile.

ANSWER 45

40. Star = 7; Tick = 8; Cross = 14; Circle = 11.

ANSWER 46

G. The internal patterns are rotated 180°.

ANSWER 47

K and O.

ANSWER 48

3. There are 4 shapes and the numbers refer to the number of shapes that surround each digit.

ANSWER 49

B. Start from top left corner and move in a vertical boustrophedon. Order is: 4 smiley face, 1 sad face, 3 straight mouth, 2 face with hair, etc.

ANSWER 50

B and H.

ANSWER 51

16. All the other numbers can be divided by 3.

ANSWER 52

Top half: + +; bottom half: + -.

ANSWER 53

E. Turn the diagram by 90° clockwise.

ANSWER 54

A and L. The numbers are 3, 4, 6 and 9.

ANSWER 55

Start at top left corner and move in a vertical boustrophedon. The order is two hearts, one square root, two crossed circles, one cross, one heart, two square roots, one crossed circle, two crosses, etc.

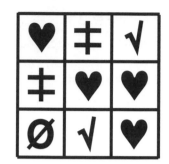

ANSWER 56

D.

ANSWER 57

5 x 4 ÷ 2 + 7 = 17.

ANSWER 58

C. The number in the middle is the sum of the squares of the numbers at the points of the triangles. C does not fit this pattern.

ANSWER 59

2. It relates to the number of shapes that enclose each figure.

ANSWER 60

Indigo and Violet (colors of the rainbow).

ANSWER 61

ANSWER 62

Top half: x ÷; bottom half: ✢ x.

ANSWER 63

B, F and N.

ANSWER 64

4 moons. Sun = 9; Moon = 5; Cloud = 3.

ANSWER 65

26. The digits in each of the other balls add up to 10.

ANSWER 66

F. The numbers made up of odd numbers are reversed.

ANSWER 67

8. Subtract the bottom left corner from the top left corner. Now subtract the bottom right corner from the top right corner, then subtract this answer from the first difference and put the number in the middle.

ANSWER 68

Three clouds and a moon. Sun = 6; Moon = 7; Cloud = 9.

ANSWER 69

The diamond. It is a closed shape.

ANSWER 70

3. The numbers in each wheel add up to 30.

ANSWER 71

The pattern is a horizontal boustrophedon starting at the top left. The sequence is: 3 stars, 2 circles, 2 squares, 3 crosses, 2 stars, 3 circles, 3 squares, 2 crosses, etc.

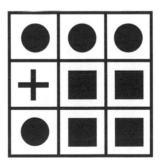

ANSWER 72

ANSWER 73

6 + 7 + 11 ÷ 3 x 2 + 5 - 12 = 9.

ANSWER 74

27. A number in the first circle is squared and the product is put in the corresponding segment of the second circle. The original number is then cubed and that product is put in the corresponding segment of the third circle.

ANSWER 75

One arrow. Oval = 1, Arrow = 2, Diamond = 3.

ANSWER 76

C. In the others the small shapes added together result in the large shape.

ANSWER 77

6:50. The minute hand moves back 5, 10 and 15 minutes, while the hour hand moves forward 1, 2 and 3 hours.

ANSWER 78

35. Star = 6; Tick = 3; Cross = 17; Circle = 12.

ANSWER 79

C. In all other cases, the biggest shape is also the smallest.

ANSWER 80

C. The minute hand moves forward 5 minutes and the hour hand moves forward 3 hours.

ANSWER 81

C. The smallest segment is rotated 90 degrees clockwise. The middle segment remains static. The largest segment is rotated 90º anti-clockwise.

ANSWER 82

B.

ANSWER 83

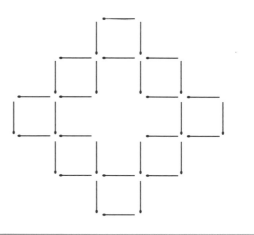

ANSWER 84

B. There is no triangle intersection on this one.

ANSWER 85

B. In all other cases the smaller circle is within the larger circle.

ANSWER 86

E. Largest shape is reflected horizontally and the size order is reversed.

ANSWER 87

B. The minute hand moves back 15 minutes and the hour hand moves forward 3 hours.

ANSWER 88

H.

ANSWER 89

A. Pattern is: 2 by arch on top, 4 by arch at right, 3 by arch on bottom, 2 by arch at left. Start at the top left corner and move down
the grid in vertical lines, reverting to the top of the next column when you reach the bottom.

ANSWER 90

B. The sequence here is minus one dot, plus two dots; the box rotates one place clockwise for each dot added or subtracted.

ANSWER 91

E and M.

ANSWER 92

R. Multiply the value of the three earliest letters, based on their value in the alphabet, by 2. The answer goes in the opposite triangle.
I (9) x 2 = 18 (R).

ANSWER 93

$4 \times 7 \div 2 + 8 + 9 \times 6 \div 3 = 62$.

ANSWER 94

42. Multiply the top top right number by the bottom left number or the top left number by the bottom right number.

ANSWER 95

D is wrong because the dot is in 3 shapes. In all the others the dot is in 2 shapes.

Medium Puzzles

This is where things start to warm up. By this point, you should have developed a reasonable feel for the types of puzzle In this book, and the basic ways in which they work. You also ought to be getting some idea about the devious minds of the puzzle authors, which will prove invaluable in the pages to come. In the pages that follow, we'll challenge you to push your brain up a gear and really start getting to grips with the puzzles.

These problems are going to test your logic, deduction, arithmetic and Ingenuity. The answers in this section are not obvious. They're designed to make you think seriously about the possible answers. You may need to forget about being able to spot solutions, and fall back on the first principles for each puzzle - how to analyse each problem, break it down to its essential components, squeeze all the information you need out of it, and put it back together again in such a way as to let you glean the answer.

Don't be disheartened if you find this section slower going than the one before. Everyone will need to take this section more seriously than the one before. Even the most hardened puzzle supremos will find themselves breaking stride to examine these problems carefully. This is where you'll find the meat of your mental workout - a few sets of these problems will leave your mind well and truly pumped.

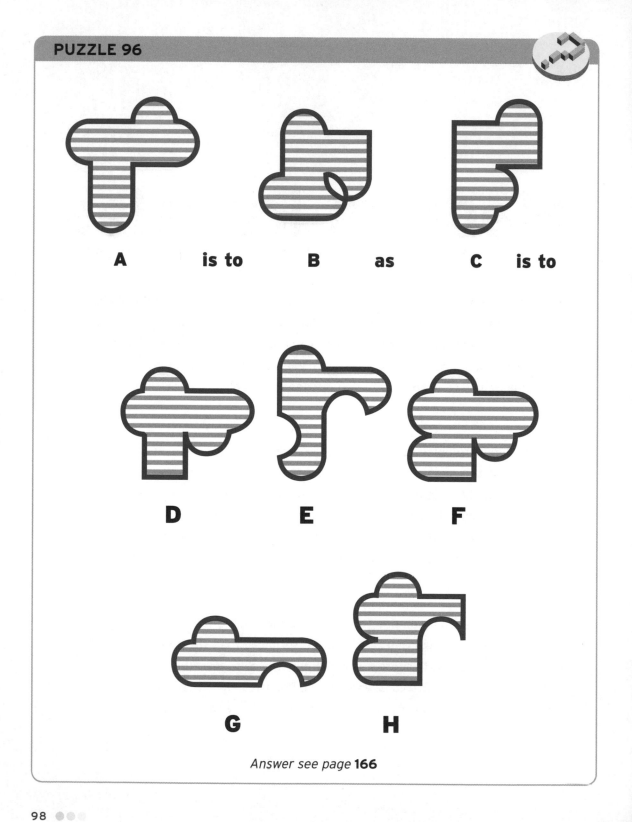

A   is to   B   as   C   is to

D   E   F

G   H

Answer see page **166**

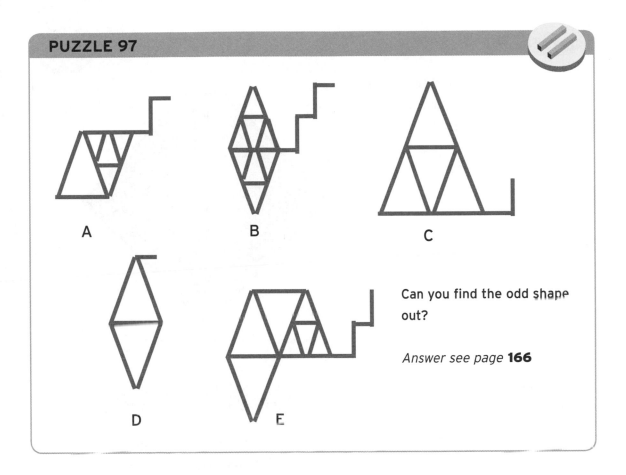

A   B   C

D   E

Can you find the odd shape out?

Answer see page **166**

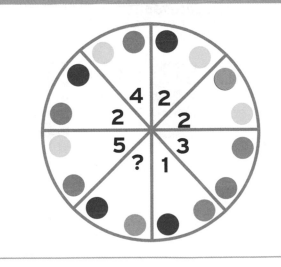

Find a number that could replace the question mark. Each color represents a number under 10.

Answer see page **166**

PUZZLE 99

The four main mathematical signs have been left out of this equation. Can you replace them?

Answer see page **166**

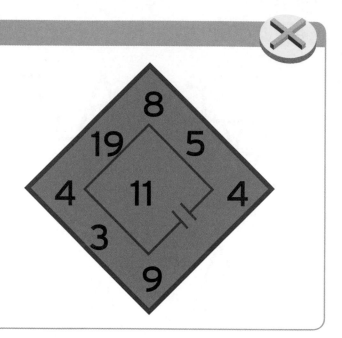

PUZZLE 100

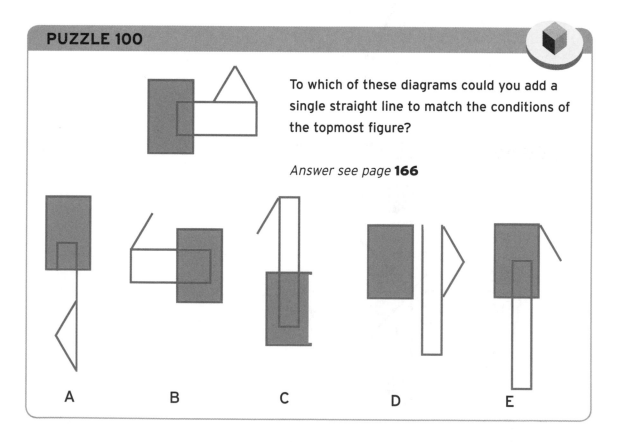

To which of these diagrams could you add a single straight line to match the conditions of the topmost figure?

Answer see page **166**

A   B   C   D   E

What is yellow worth?

Answer see page **166**

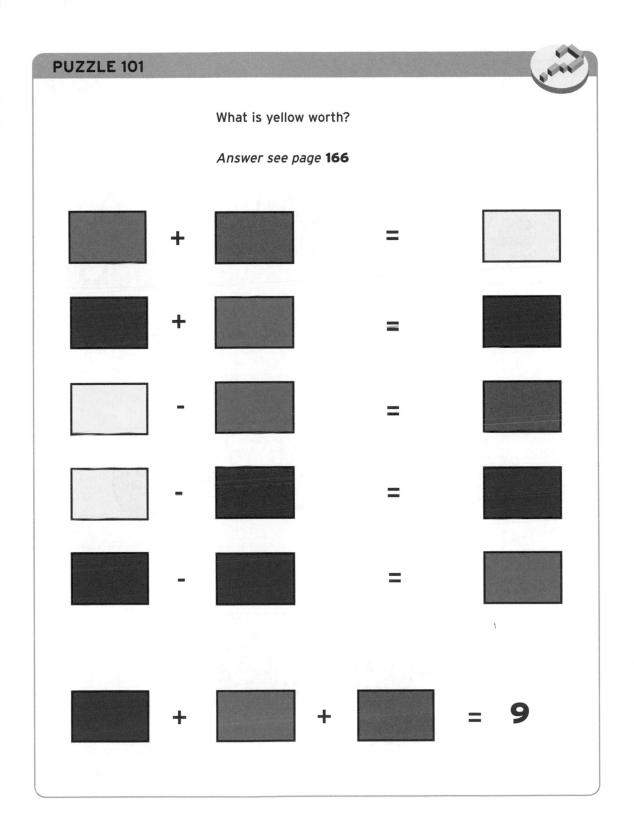

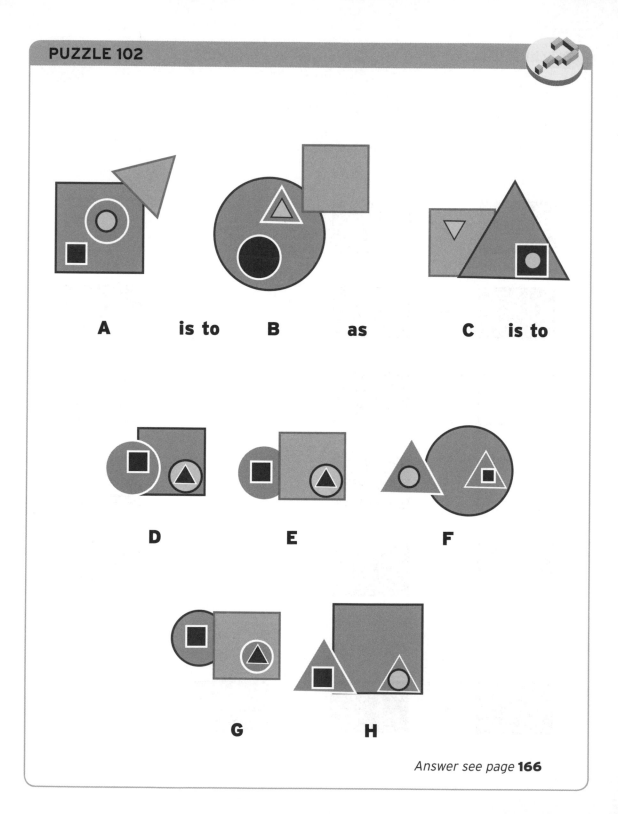

A   is to   B   as   C   is to

D   E   F

G   H

*Answer see page **166***

PUZZLE 103

Can you work out which number the missing hand on clock 4 should point to?

Answer see page **166**

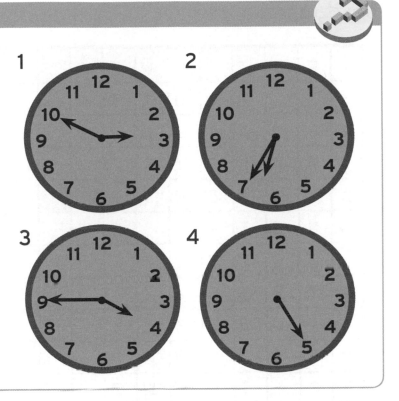

PUZZLE 104

Can you work out the logic behind this square and fill in the missing section?

Answer see page **166**

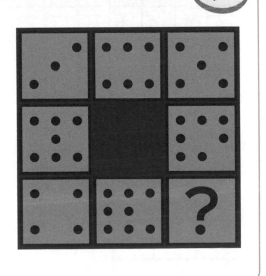

Z	R	T	T	U	W	W	Z	Z	S	Z	R	T	T	U	W
S	Z	Z	W	W	U	T	T	R	Z	S	Z	Z	W	W	U
Z	S	Z	R	T	T	U	W	W	Z	Z	S	Z	R	T	T
Z	W	W	U	T	T	R	Z	S	Z	Z	W	W	U	T	T
W	Z	Z	S	Z	R	T	T				Z	Z	S	Z	R
W	U	T	T	R	Z	S	Z				U	T	T	R	Z
U	W	W	Z	Z	S	Z	R				W	W	Z	Z	S
T	T	R	Z	S	Z	Z	W	W	U	T	T	R	Z	S	Z
T	T	U	W	W	Z	Z	S	Z	R	T	T	U	W	W	Z
R	Z	S	Z	Z	W	W	U	T	T	R	Z	S	Z	Z	W
Z	R	T	T	U	W	W	Z	Z	S	Z	R	T	T	U	W
S	Z	Z	W	W	U	T	T	R	Z	S	Z	Z	W	W	U
Z	S	Z	R	T	T	U	W	W	Z	Z	S	Z	R	T	T
Z	W	W	U	T	T	R	Z	S	Z	Z	W	W	U	T	T
W	Z	Z	S	Z	R	T	T	U	W	W	Z	Z	S	Z	R
W	U	T	T	R	Z	S	Z	Z	W	W	U	T	T	R	Z

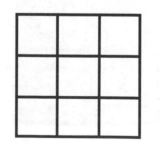

Can you spot the pattern of this grid and complete the missing section?

Answer see page **166**

PUZZLE 106

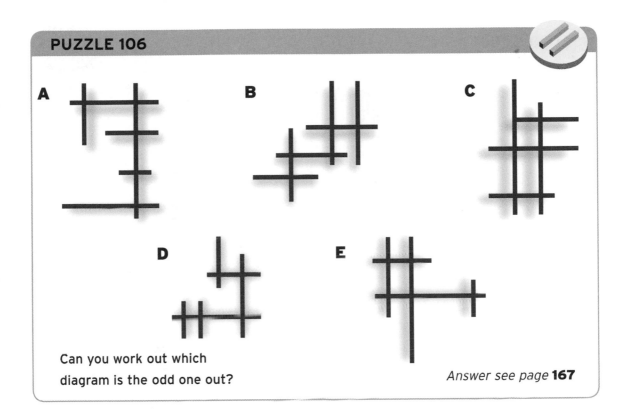

A

B

C

D

E

Can you work out which diagram is the odd one out?

Answer see page **167**

PUZZLE 107

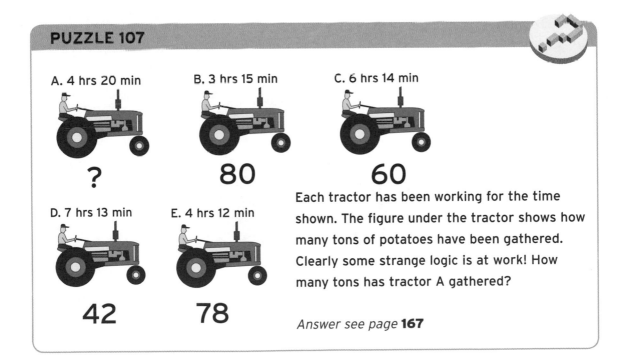

A. 4 hrs 20 min

?

B. 3 hrs 15 min

80

C. 6 hrs 14 min

60

D. 7 hrs 13 min

42

E. 4 hrs 12 min

78

Each tractor has been working for the time shown. The figure under the tractor shows how many tons of potatoes have been gathered. Clearly some strange logic is at work! How many tons has tractor A gathered?

Answer see page **167**

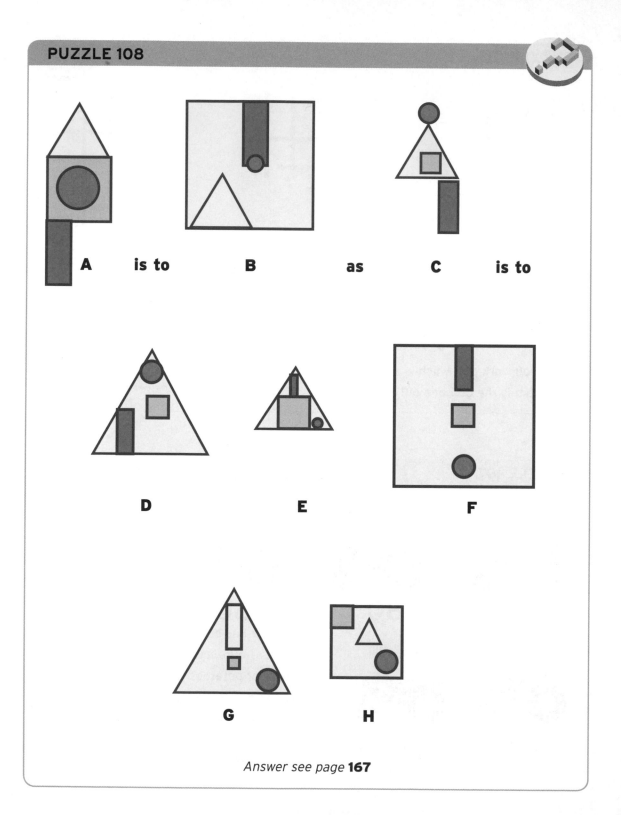

A   is to   B   as   C   is to

D   E   F

G   H

Answer see page 167

PUZZLE 109

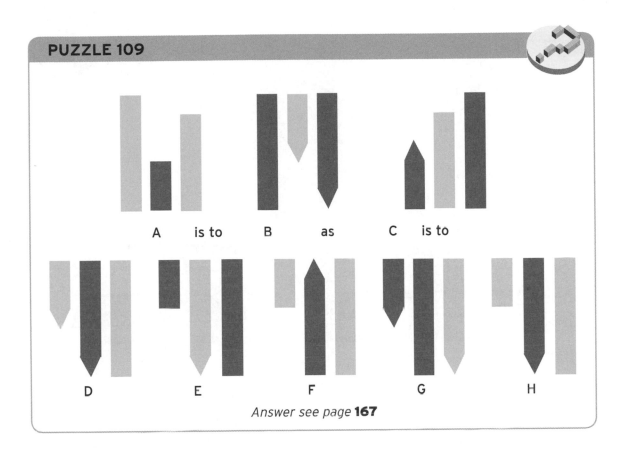

A   is to   B   as   C   is to

D   E   F   G   H

Answer see page **167**

PUZZLE 110

Can you spot the cube that cannot be made
from the layout below?

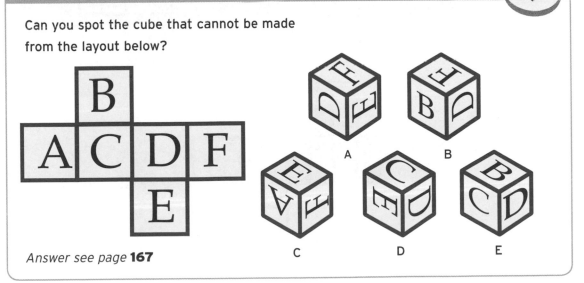

Answer see page **167**

PUZZLE 111

Which of these layouts could be used to make the cube to the right?

Answer see page **167**

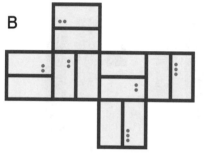

A
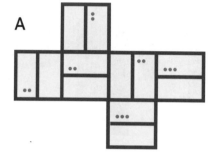

B
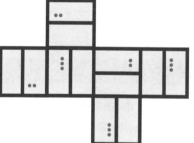

C
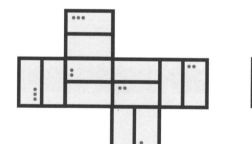

D

E
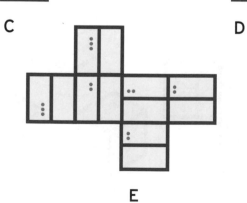

PUZZLE 112

If you know that the answer forms a well-known sequence, can you work out how much each shape is worth?

*Answer see page **167***

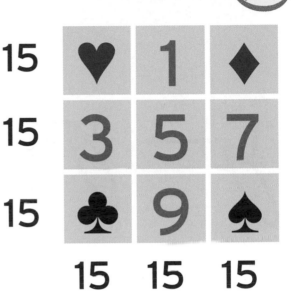

PUZZLE 113

Can you work out what the next matchstick man in this series should look like?

*Answer see page **167***

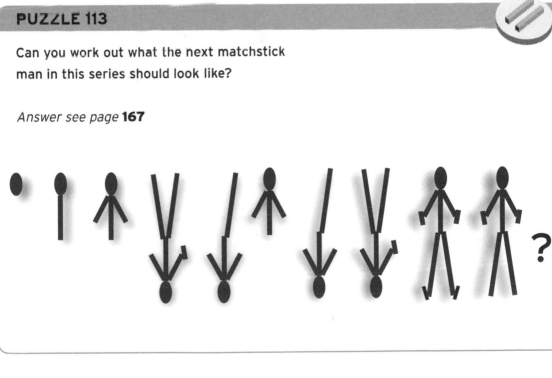

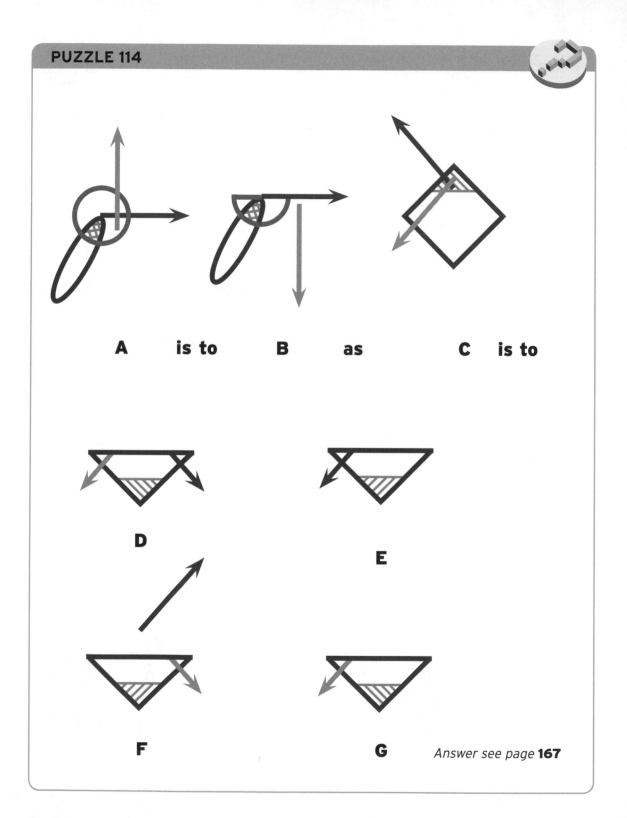

A   is to   B   as   C   is to

D

E

F

G

Answer see page **167**

PUZZLE 115

Which of these columns would continue the sequence to the right?

Answer see page **167**

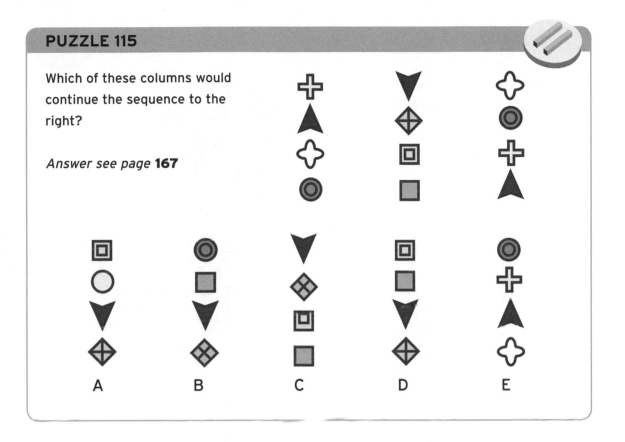

A   B   C   D   E

PUZZLE 116

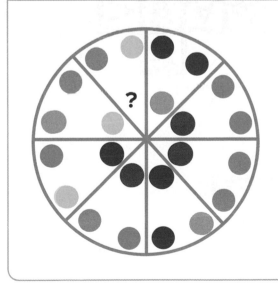

Find a number that could replace the question mark. Each color represents a number under 10.

Answer see page **167**

Which of the following layouts could
be used to make the above cube?

Answer see page **167**

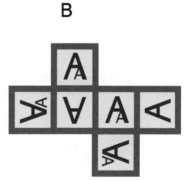

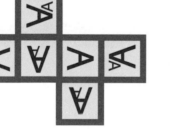

A

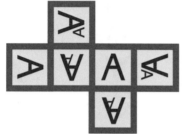

B

C

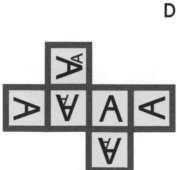

D

E

PUZZLE 118

Can you work out which symbol is
the odd one out?

Answer see page **167**

A   B   C   D   E

PUZZLE 119

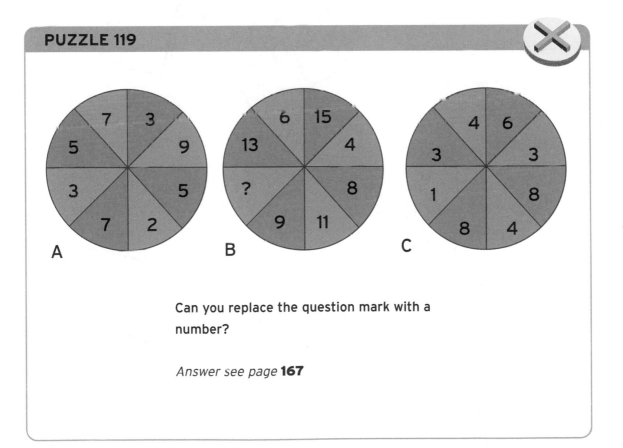

A   B   C

Can you replace the question mark with a
number?

Answer see page **167**

Can you work out which is
the odd diagram out?

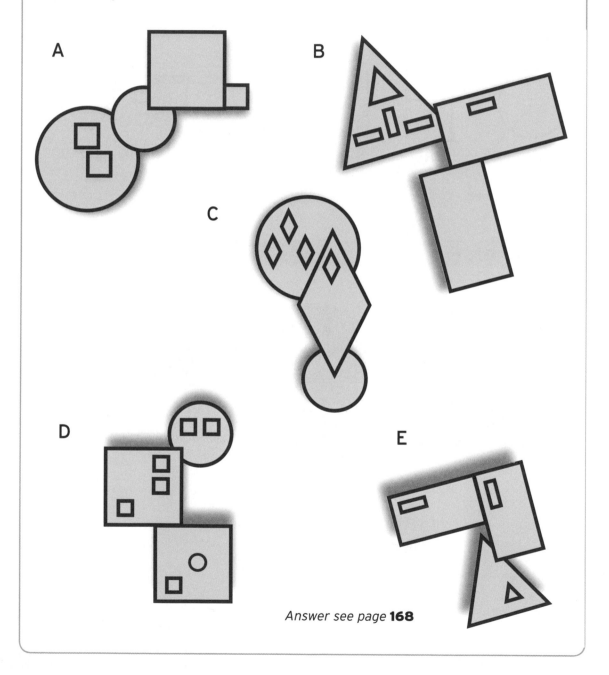

Answer see page **168**

PUZZLE 121

Can you work out which of these symbols comes next in this sequence?

Answer see page **168**

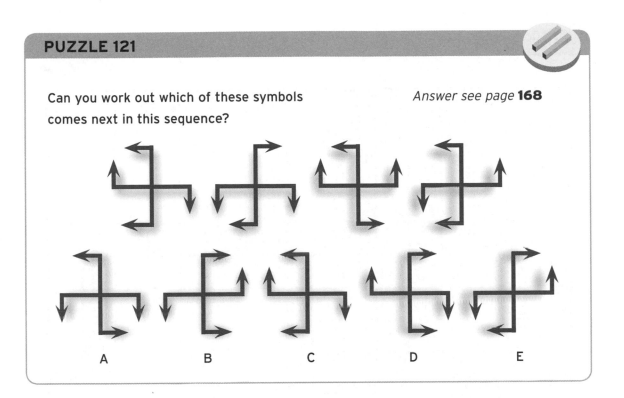

A   B   C   D   E

PUZZLE 122

Can you work out the logic behind this square and find the missing number?

Answer see page **168**

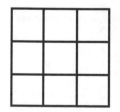

Can you work out what pattern this grid follows and complete the missing section?

Answer see page **168**

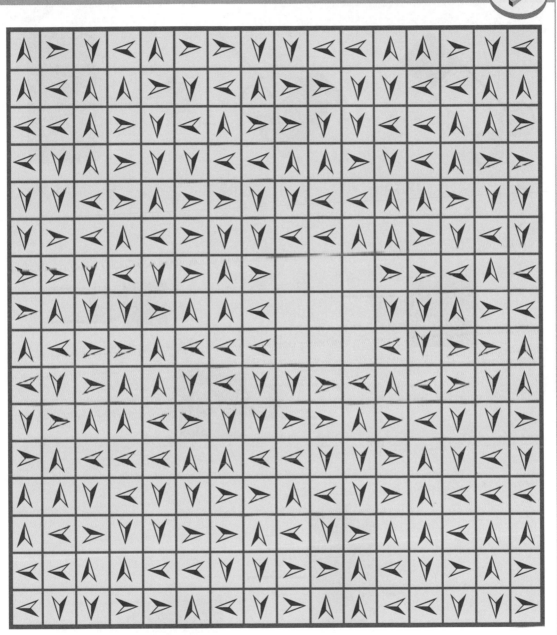

Can you work out the reasoning behind this
grid and complete the missing section?

Answer see page **168**

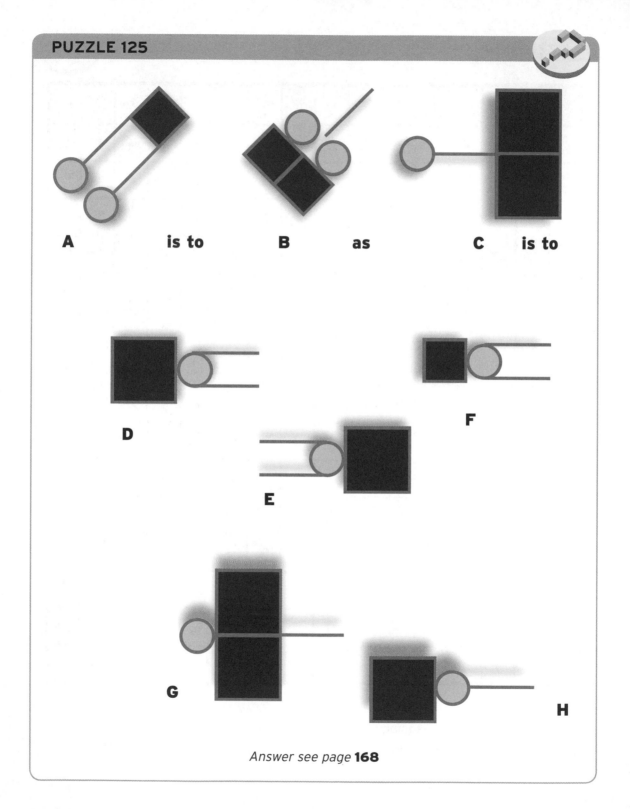

A   is to   B   as   C   is to

D

F

E

G

H

Answer see page **168**

PUZZLE 126

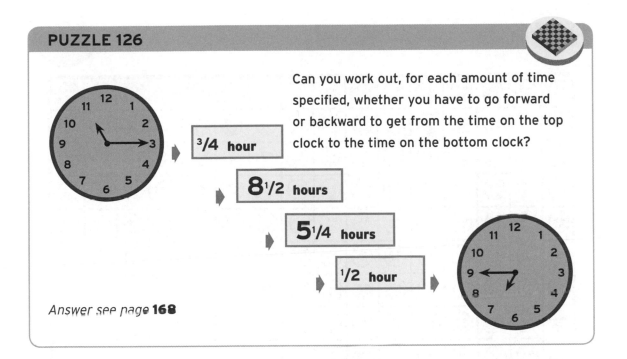

Can you work out, for each amount of time specified, whether you have to go forward or backward to get from the time on the top clock to the time on the bottom clock?

³/4 hour

8¹/2 hours

5¹/4 hours

¹/2 hour

Answer see page **168**

PUZZLE 127

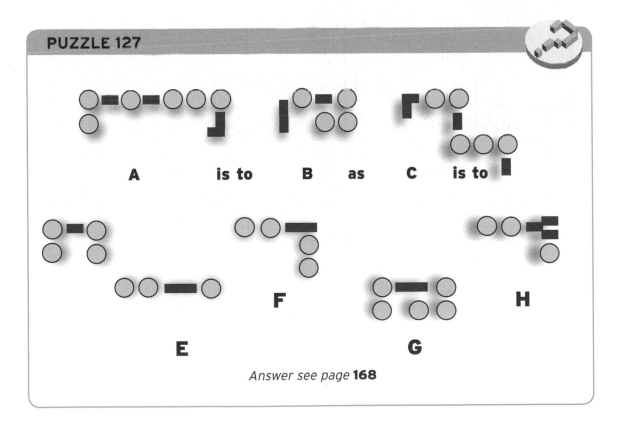

A   is to   B   as   C   is to

E

F

G

H

Answer see page **168**

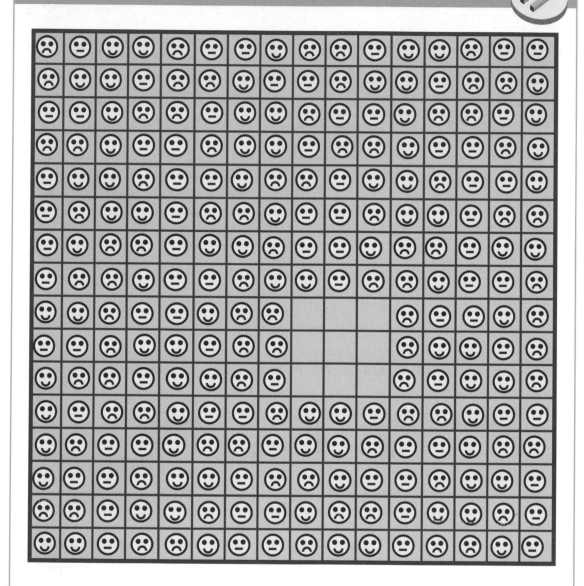

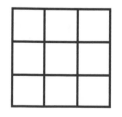

This grid is made up according to a certain pattern. Can you work it out and fill in the missing section?

Answer see page **168**

PUZZLE 129

Can you work out how many
rectangles altogether can be found
in this diagram?

Answer see page **169**

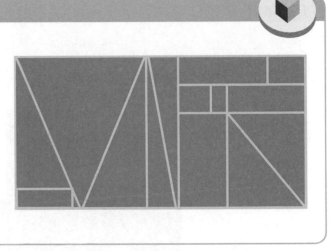

PUZZLE 130

Can you work out which
shape is the odd one out?

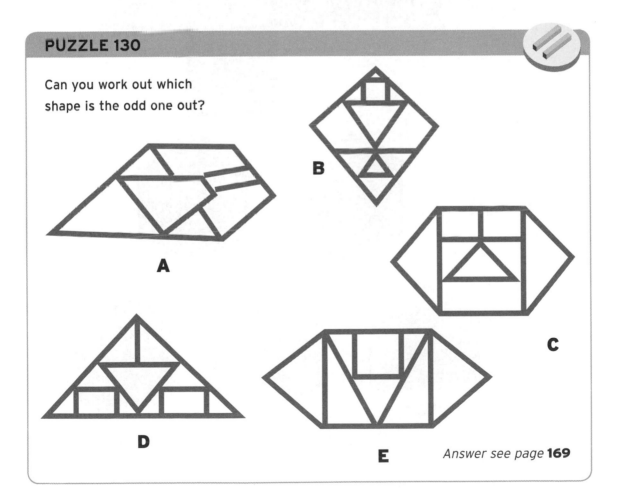

A

B

C

D

E

Answer see page **169**

Can you work out which of these cubes
cannot be made from the layout below?

*Answer see page **169***

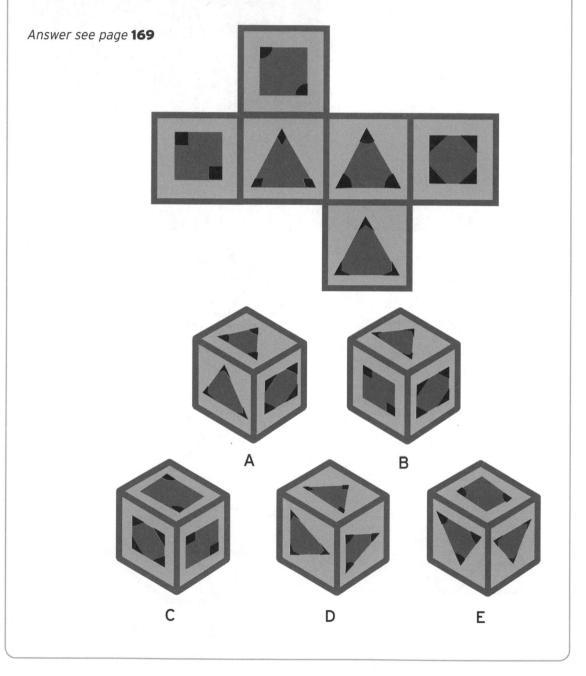

A

B

C

D

E

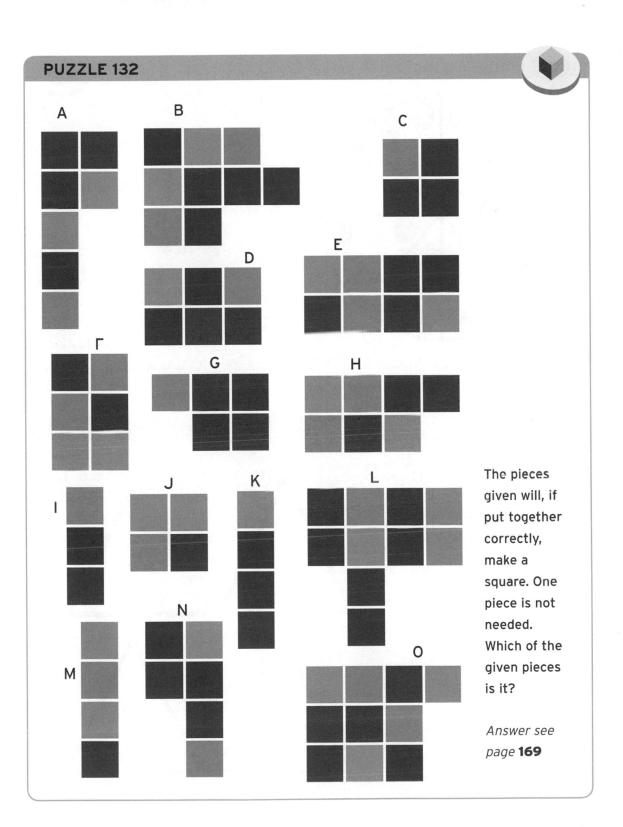

The pieces given will, if put together correctly, make a square. One piece is not needed. Which of the given pieces is it?

Answer see page **169**

PUZZLE 133

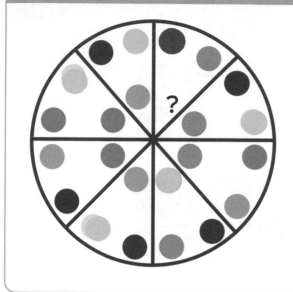

Which color is the circle that replaces the question mark?

Answer see page **169**

PUZZLE 134

Find a number that could replace the question mark. Each color represents a number under 10.

Answer see page **169**

11

13

14

?

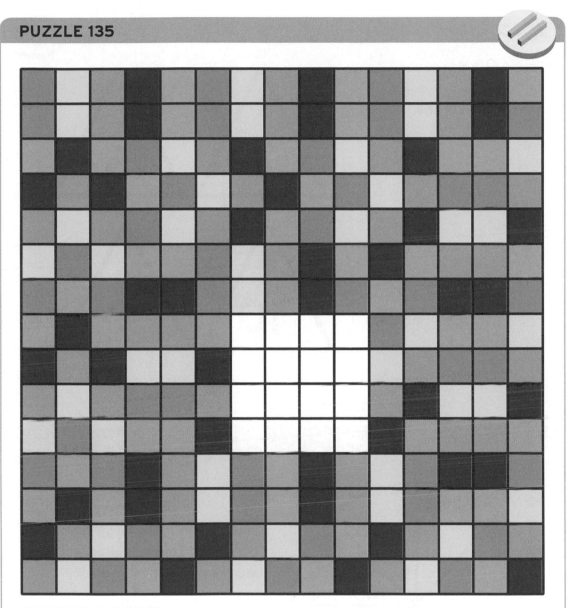

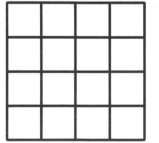

This square is drawn according to a certain logic. If you can work out what the system is you should be able to fill in the missing area.

Answer see page **169**

PUZZLE 136

Find the missing number.

Answer see page **169**

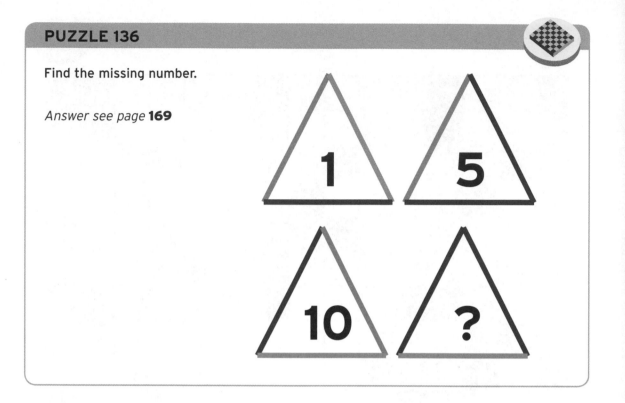

PUZZLE 137

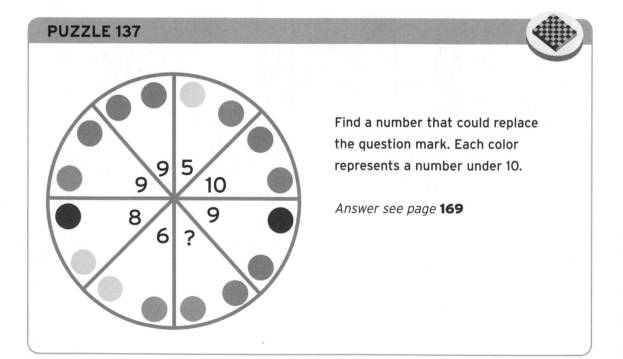

Find a number that could replace the question mark. Each color represents a number under 10.

Answer see page **169**

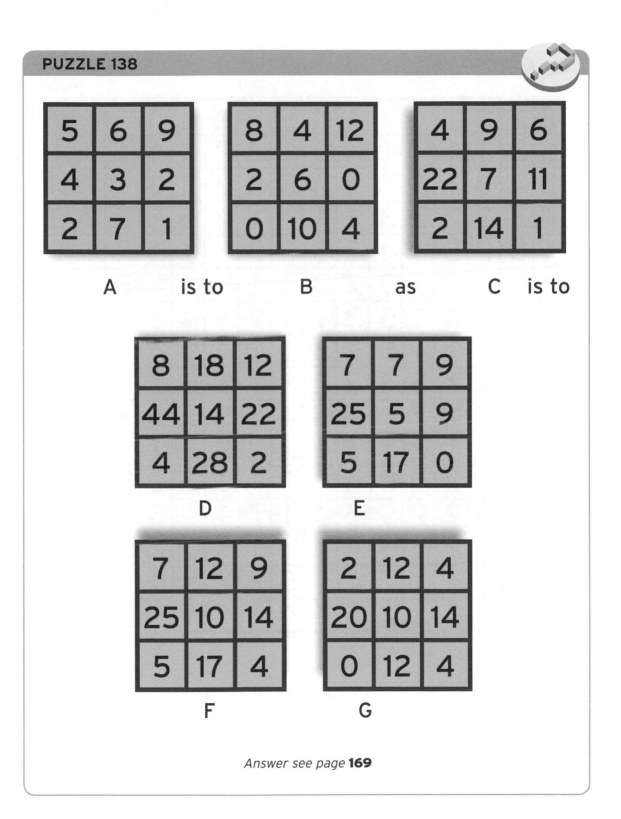

A   is to   B   as   C   is to

D

E

F

G

Answer see page **169**

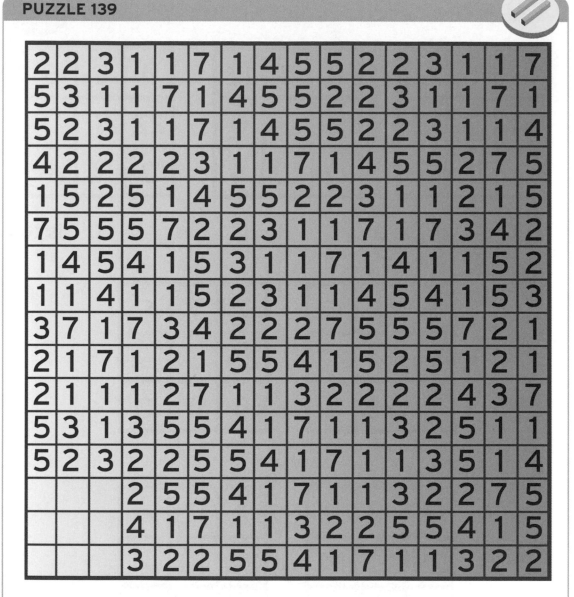

2	2	3	1	1	7	1	4	5	5	2	2	3	1	1	7
5	3	1	1	7	1	4	5	5	2	2	3	1	1	7	1
5	2	3	1	1	7	1	4	5	5	2	2	3	1	1	4
4	2	2	2	3	1	1	7	1	4	5	5	2	7	5	
1	5	2	5	1	4	5	5	2	2	3	1	1	2	1	5
7	5	5	5	7	2	2	3	1	1	7	1	7	3	4	2
1	4	5	4	1	5	3	1	1	7	1	4	1	1	5	2
1	1	4	1	1	5	2	3	1	1	4	5	4	1	5	3
3	7	1	7	3	4	2	2	2	7	5	5	5	7	2	1
2	1	7	1	2	1	5	5	4	1	5	2	5	1	2	1
2	1	1	1	2	7	1	1	3	2	2	2	2	4	3	7
5	3	1	3	5	5	4	1	7	1	1	3	2	5	1	1
5	2	3	2	2	5	5	4	1	7	1	1	3	5	1	4
			2	5	5	4	1	7	1	1	3	2	2	7	5
			4	1	7	1	1	3	2	2	5	5	4	1	5
			3	2	2	5	5	4	1	7	1	1	3	2	2

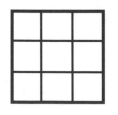

Can you work out the reasoning behind this grid and complete the missing section?

Answer see page **169**

PUZZLE 140

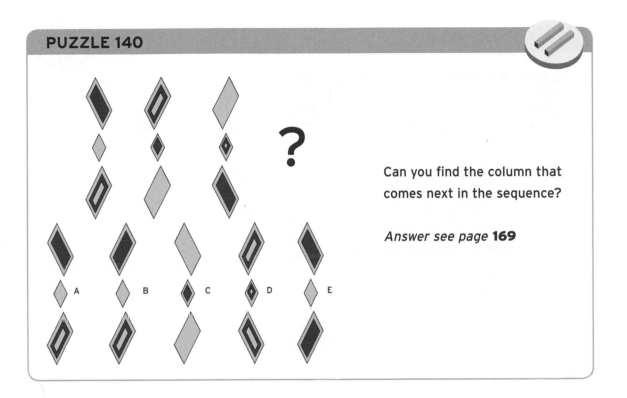

Can you find the column that comes next in the sequence?

Answer see page **169**

PUZZLE 141

Can you work out what the next fish in this sequence should look like?

Answer see page **170**

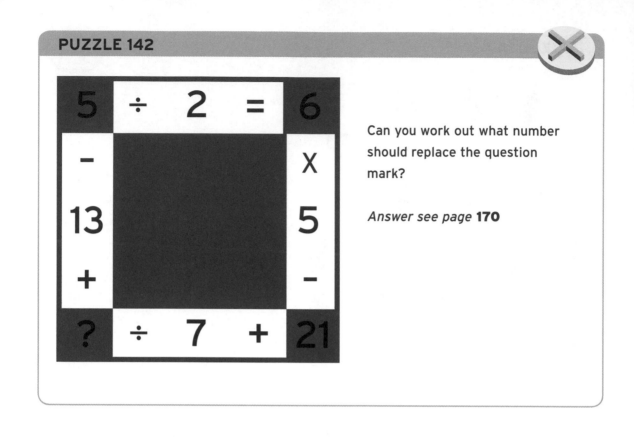

Can you work out what number should replace the question mark?

Answer see page **170**

The weight of each suitcase is shown.
Which is the odd one out?

Answer see page **170**

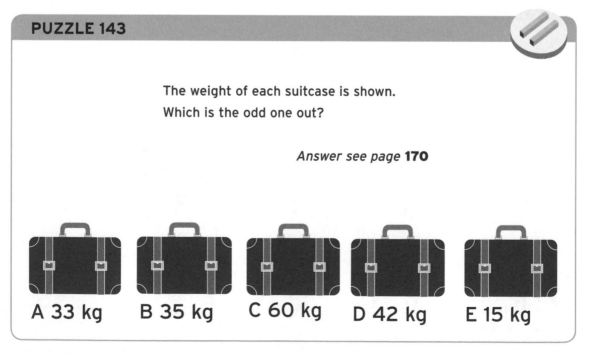

A 33 kg   B 35 kg   C 60 kg   D 42 kg   E 15 kg

PUZZLE 144

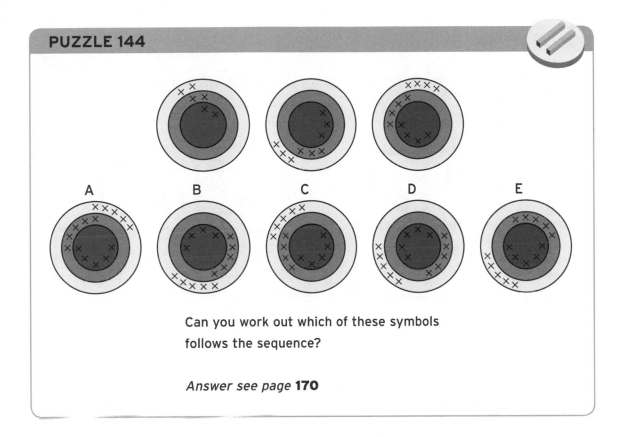

Can you work out which of these symbols follows the sequence?

Answer see page **170**

PUZZLE 145

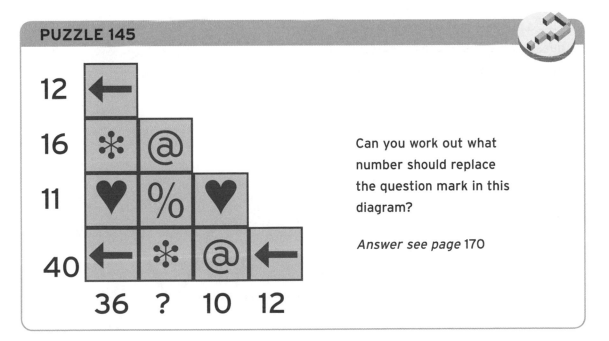

Can you work out what number should replace the question mark in this diagram?

Answer see page 170

PUZZLE 146

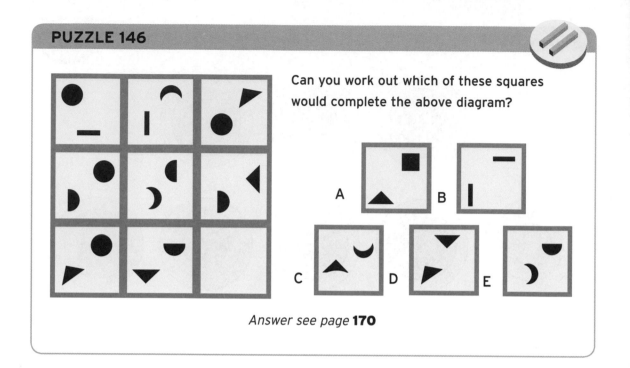

Can you work out which of these squares would complete the above diagram?

Answer see page **170**

PUZZLE 147

Find a number that could replace the question mark. Each color represents a number under 10.

Answer see page **170**

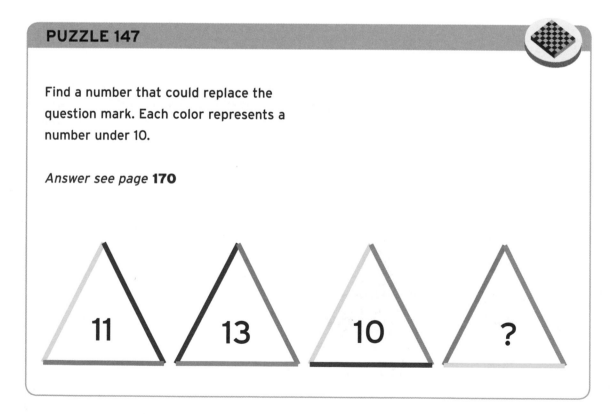

PUZZLE 148

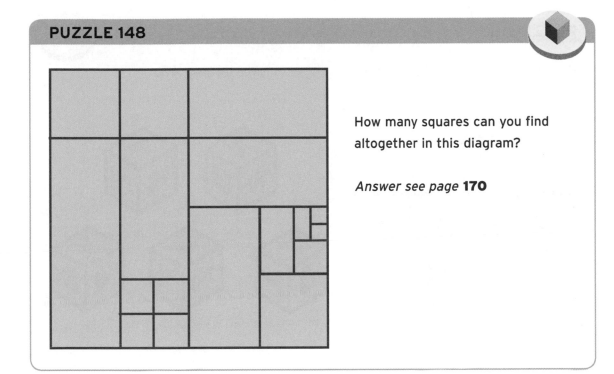

How many squares can you find altogether in this diagram?

Answer see page **170**

PUZZLE 149

Which of these triangles is the odd one out? Their color is a factor.

Answer see page **170**

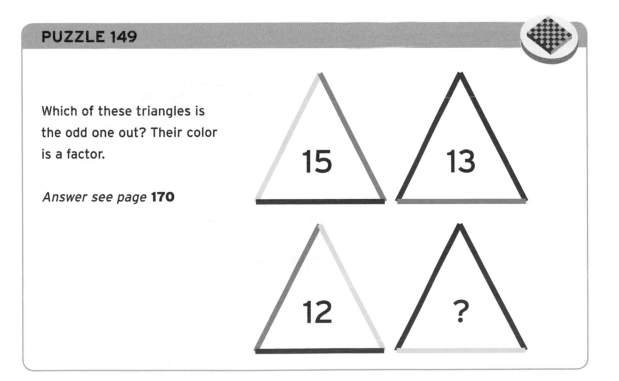

PUZZLE 150

Can you spot the cube that cannot be made from the layout below?

Answer see page **170**

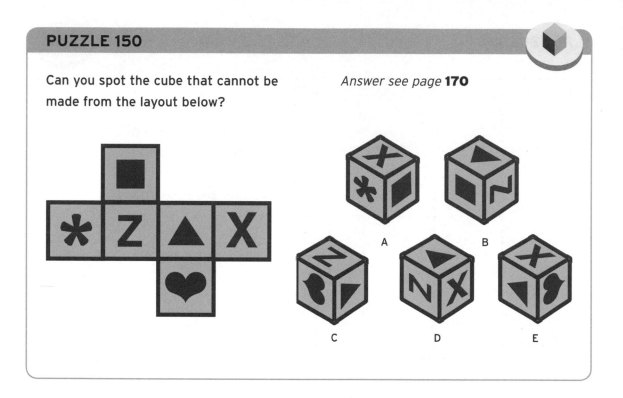

PUZZLE 151

Find a number that could replace the question mark. Each color represents a number under 10.

Answer see page **170**

PUZZLE 152

12   19

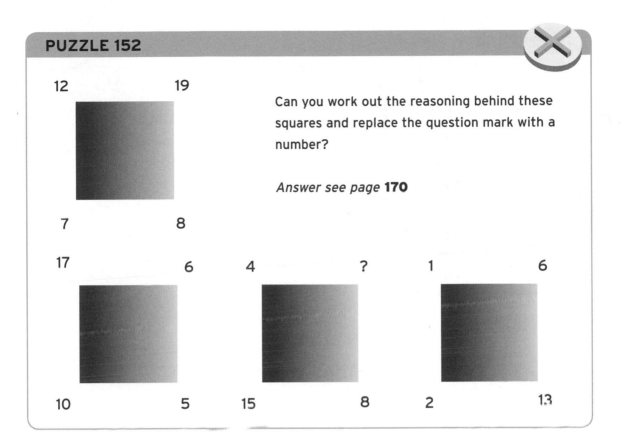

7   8

17   6   4   ?   1   6

10   5   15   8   2   13

Can you work out the reasoning behind these squares and replace the question mark with a number?

Answer see page **170**

PUZZLE 153

Can you find the number that should replace the question mark?

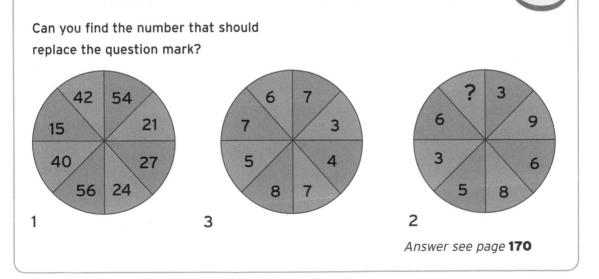

1   3   2

Answer see page **170**

PUZZLE 154

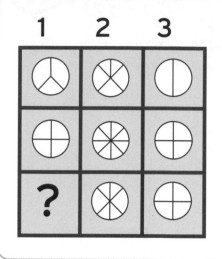

Can you work out the reasoning behind this square and replace the question mark with the correct shape?

Answer see page **170**

PUZZLE 155

Five cyclists are taking part in a race. The number of each rider and his cycling time are related to each other. Can you work out the number of the last cyclist?

Answer see page **171**

No. 9

Takes 1 hr 35

No. 10

Takes 1 hr 43

No. 11

Takes 1 hr 52

No. 14

Takes 2 hr 27

No. ?

Takes 2 hr 33

PUZZLE 156

Can you work out which diagram would continue the series?

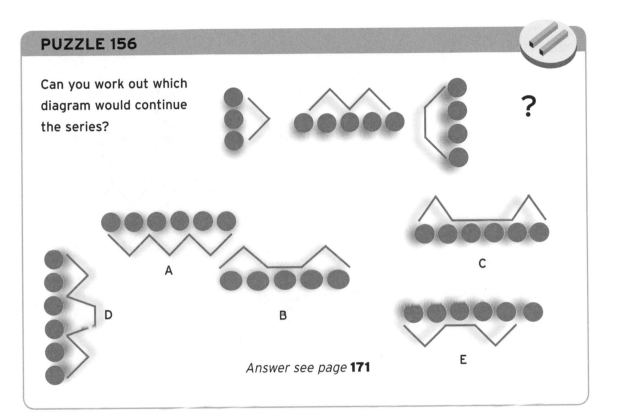

Answer see page **171**

PUZZLE 157

Find the missing number.

Answer see page **171**

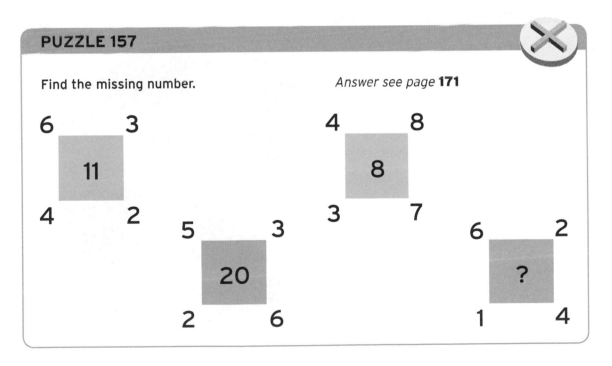

PUZZLE 158

Which of these cubes can be made from the above layout?

Answer see page **171**

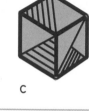

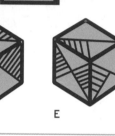

A   B   C   D   E

PUZZLE 159

Can you work out the reasoning behind this wheel and replace the question mark with a number?

Answer see page **171**

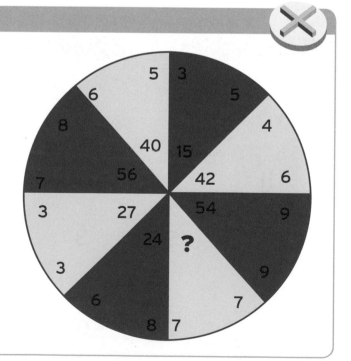

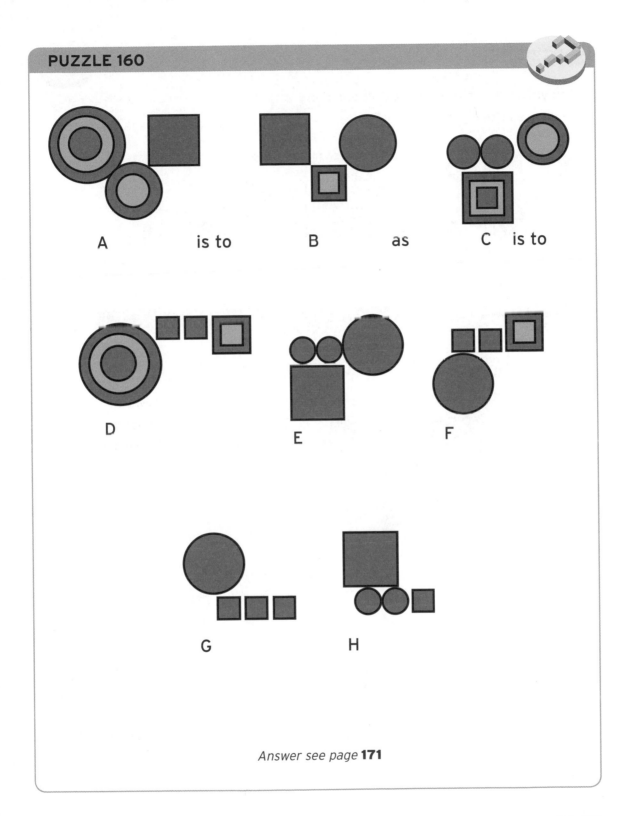

A   is to   B   as   C   is to

D   E   F

G   H

Answer see page **171**

PUZZLE 161

Can you work out what the next grid in the sequence below should look like?

Answer see page **171**

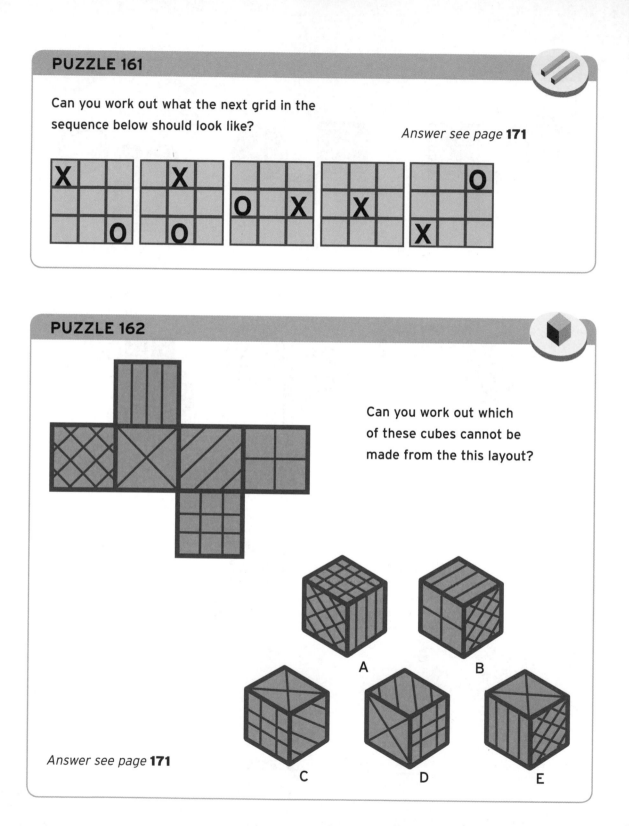

PUZZLE 162

Can you work out which of these cubes cannot be made from the this layout?

A

B

C

D

E

Answer see page **171**

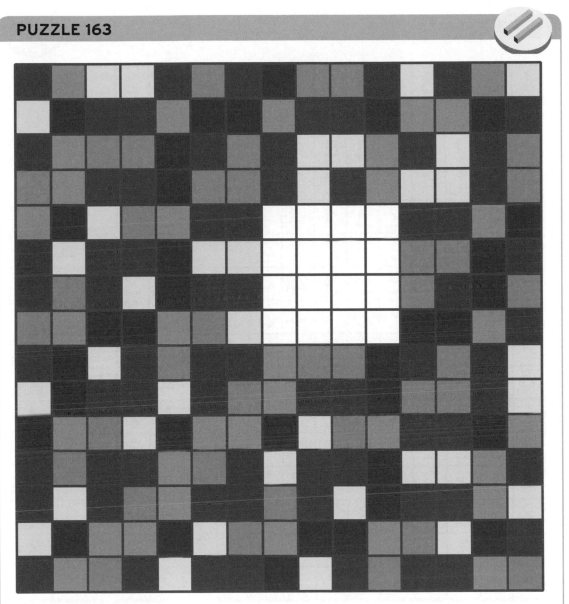

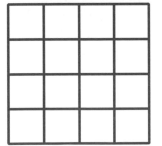

The small squares form a logical sequence. If you can discover what that sequence is you should be able to complete the missing section.

Answer see page **171**

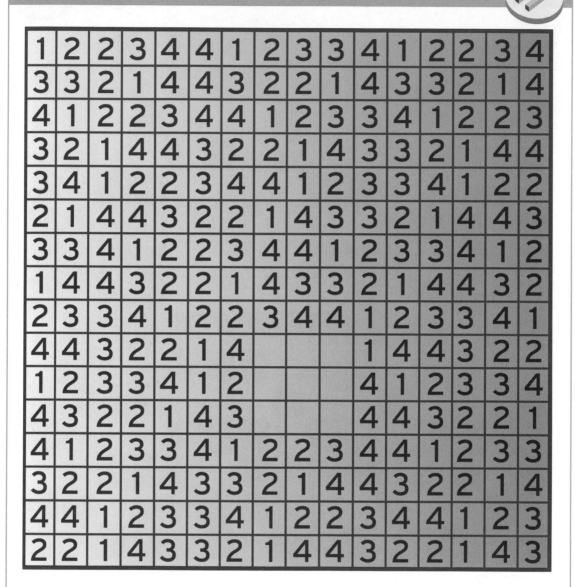

1	2	2	3	4	4	1	2	3	3	4	1	2	2	3	4
3	3	2	1	4	4	3	2	2	1	4	3	3	2	1	4
4	1	2	2	3	4	4	1	2	3	3	4	1	2	2	3
3	2	1	4	4	3	2	2	1	4	3	3	2	1	4	4
3	4	1	2	2	3	4	4	1	2	3	3	4	1	2	2
2	1	4	4	3	2	2	1	4	3	3	2	1	4	4	3
3	3	4	1	2	2	3	4	4	1	2	3	3	4	1	2
1	4	4	3	2	2	1	4	3	3	2	1	4	4	3	2
2	3	3	4	1	2	2	3	4	4	1	2	3	3	4	1
4	4	3	2	2	1	4				1	4	4	3	2	2
1	2	3	3	4	1	2				4	1	2	3	3	4
4	3	2	2	1	4	3				4	4	3	2	2	1
4	1	2	3	3	4	1	2	2	3	4	4	1	2	3	3
3	2	2	1	4	3	3	2	1	4	4	3	2	2	1	4
4	4	1	2	3	3	4	1	2	2	3	4	4	1	2	3
2	2	1	4	3	3	2	1	4	4	3	2	2	1	4	3

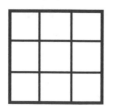

Can you work out the reasoning behind this grid and complete the missing section?

*Answer see page **171***

PUZZLE 165

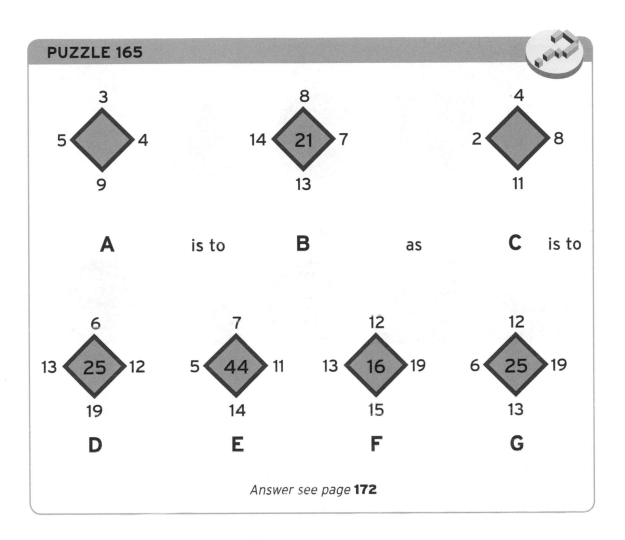

3
5 ◇ 4
9

A is to

8
14 ◇ 21 ◇ 7
13

B as

4
2 ◇ 8
11

C is to

6
13 ◇ 25 ◇ 12
19

D

7
5 ◇ 44 ◇ 11
14

E

12
13 ◇ 16 ◇ 19
15

F

12
6 ◇ 25 ◇ 19
13

G

*Answer see page **172***

PUZZLE 166

Each horse carries a weight handicap.
Can you work out the number of the final horse?   *Answer see page **172***

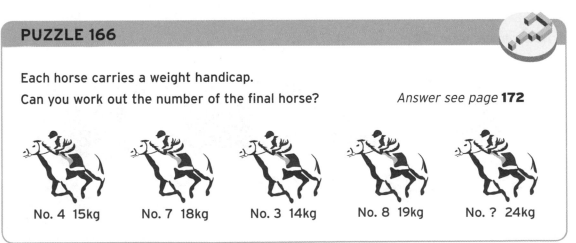

No. 4 15kg   No. 7 18kg   No. 3 14kg   No. 8 19kg   No. ? 24kg

PUZZLE 167

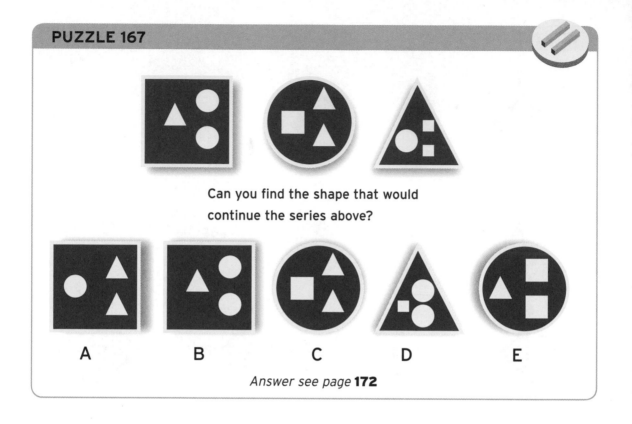

Can you find the shape that would continue the series above?

A   B   C   D   E

Answer see page **172**

PUZZLE 168

Can you work out the reasoning behind these squares and find the missing number?

Answer see page **172**

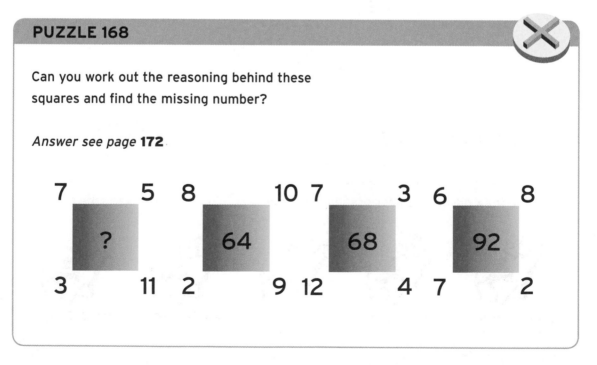

PUZZLE 169

All these bikes took part in an overnight race. Something really weird happened! The start and finish times of the bikes became mathematically linked. If you can discover the link you should be able to decide when bike D finished.

Answer see page **172**

A START 3:15
FINISH 2:06

B START 3:20
FINISH 1:09

C START 5:24
FINISH 2:11

D START 7:35
FINISH ?

E START 6:28
FINISH 4:22

PUZZLE 170

To which of these diagrams could you add a circle to match the conditions of the figure at right?

Answer see page **172**

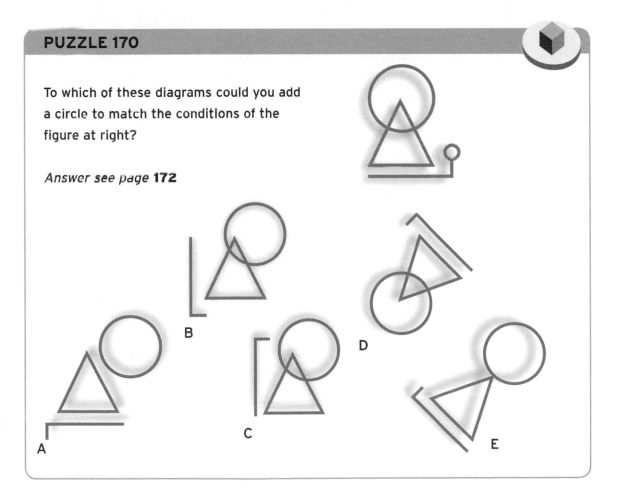

A

B

C

D

E

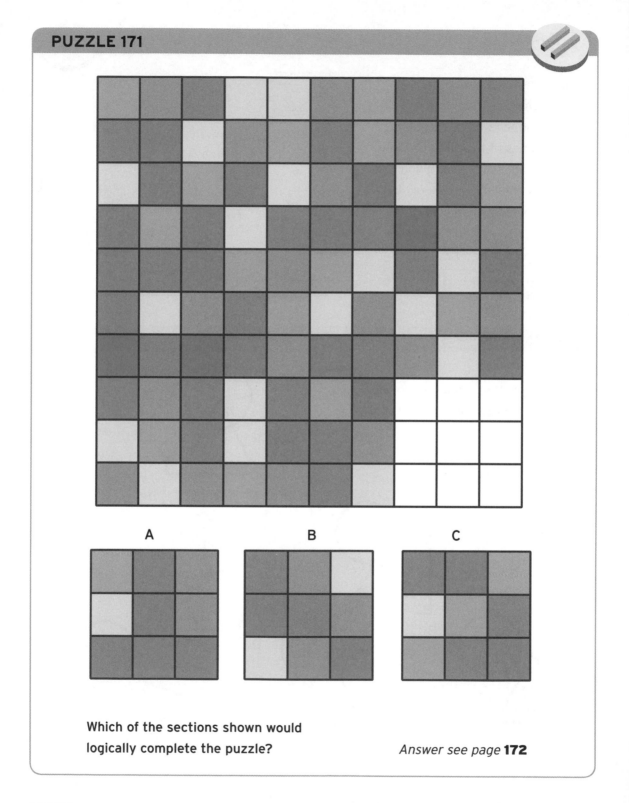

A
B
C

Which of the sections shown would
logically complete the puzzle?

*Answer see page **172***

PUZZLE 172

Which of these shapes fits to
complete the polygon?

Answer see page **172**

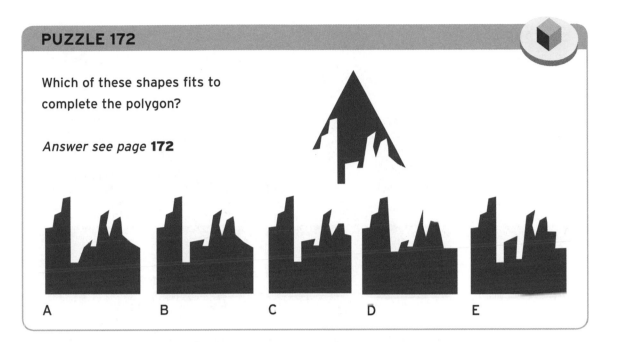

A   B   C   D   E

PUZZLE 173

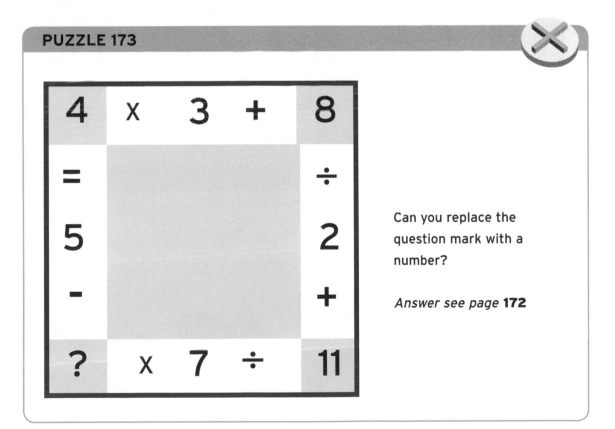

Can you replace the
question mark with a
number?

Answer see page **172**

PUZZLE 174

Can you work out which of these squares is the odd one out?

Answer see page **172**

A   B   C   D   E

F   G   H   I   J

K   L   M   N   O

PUZZLE 175

Can you find the odd shape out?

Answer see page **172**

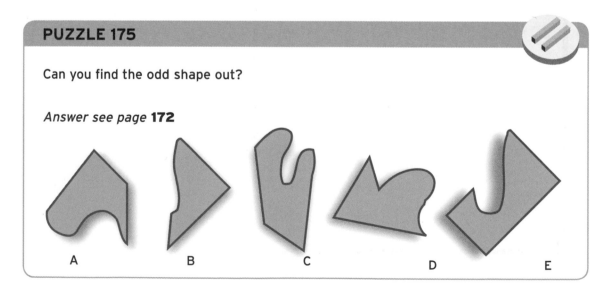

A   B   C   D   E

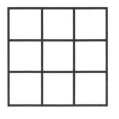

Can you work out the pattern sequence and
fill in the missing section?

Answer see page **172**

PUZZLE 177

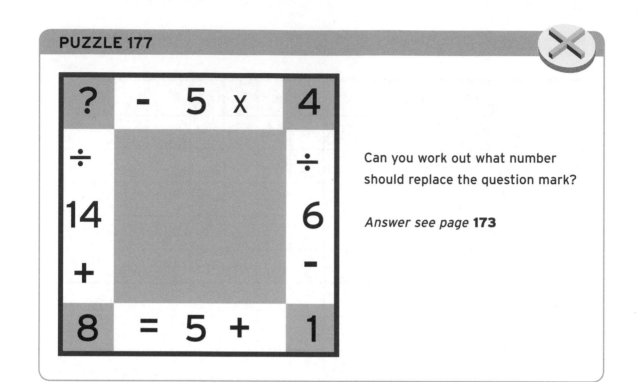

Can you work out what number should replace the question mark?

Answer see page **173**

PUZZLE 178

Can you work out what number should replace the question mark?

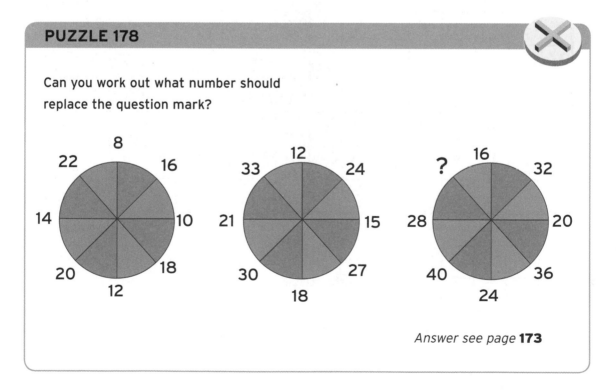

Answer see page **173**

PUZZLE 179

Which cube can be made from this layout?

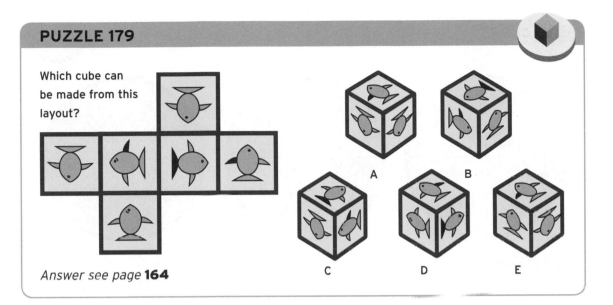

A

B

C

D

E

Answer see page **164**

PUZZLE 180

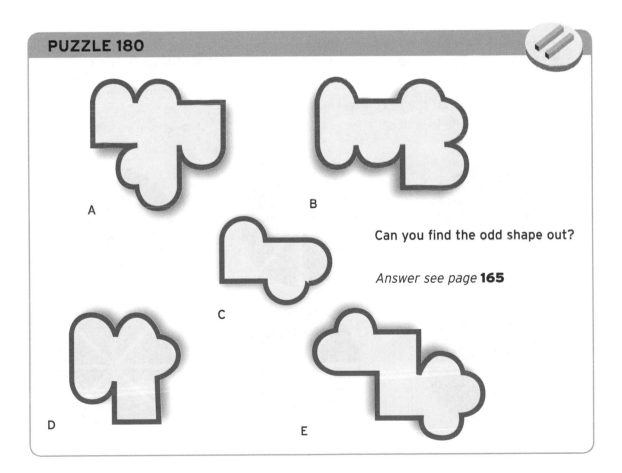

A

B

C

Can you find the odd shape out?

Answer see page **165**

D

E

PUZZLE 181

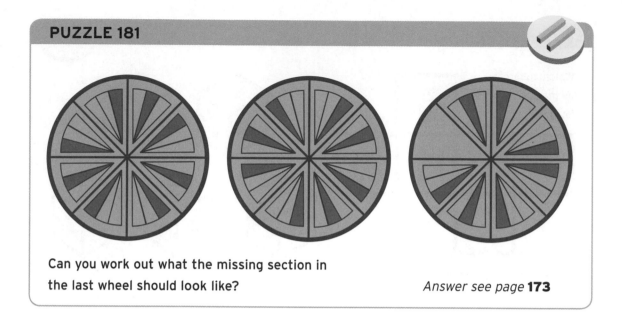

Can you work out what the missing section in the last wheel should look like?

Answer see page **173**

PUZZLE 182

Can you work out what the next wheel in this sequence should look like?

Answer see page **173**

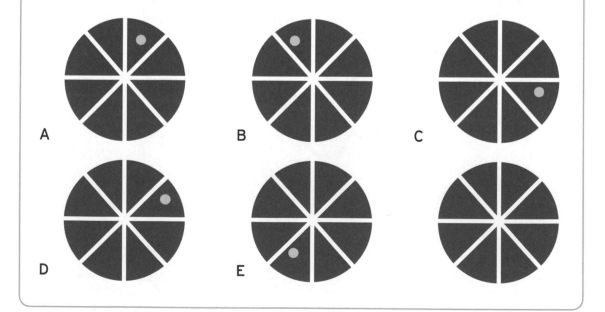

PUZZLE 183

A is to   B as   C is to

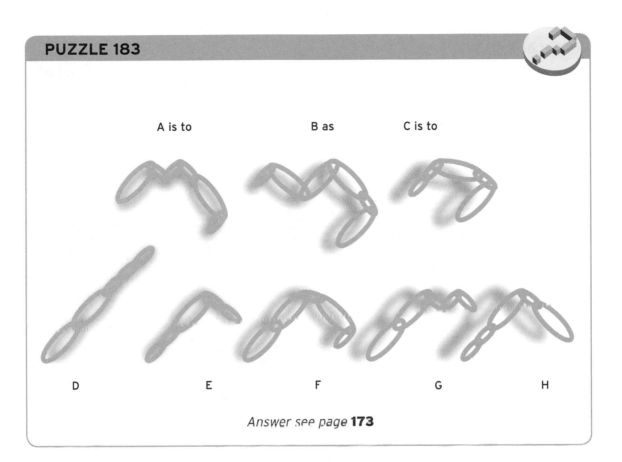

D   E   F   G   H

Answer see page **173**

PUZZLE 184

Can you work out the reasoning behind these
squares and find the number that should
replace the question mark?

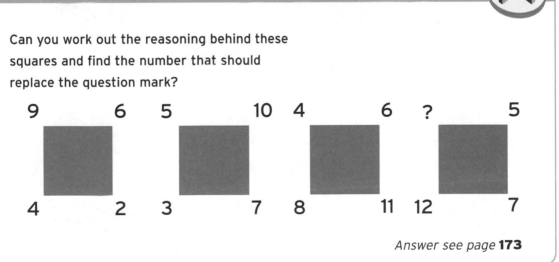

Answer see page **173**

PUZZLE 185

Can you find the odd shape out?

Answer see page **173**

A   B   C   E   D

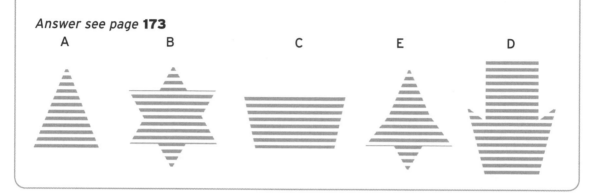

PUZZLE 186

Can you find the odd diagram out?

Answer see page **173**

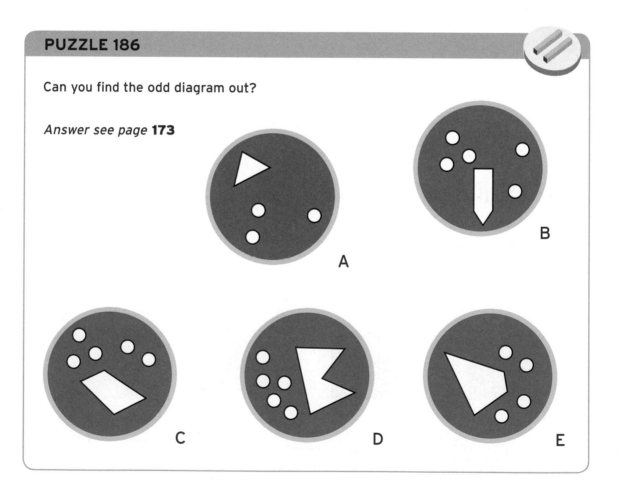

PUZZLE 187

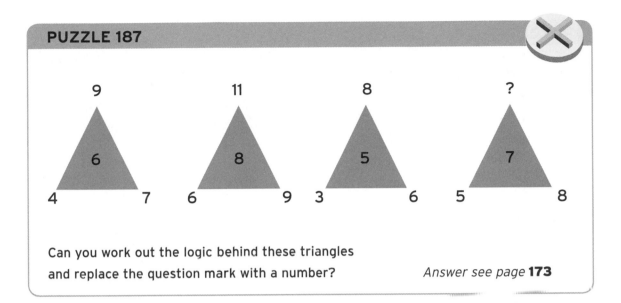

Can you work out the logic behind these triangles
and replace the question mark with a number?

Answer see page **173**

PUZZLE 188

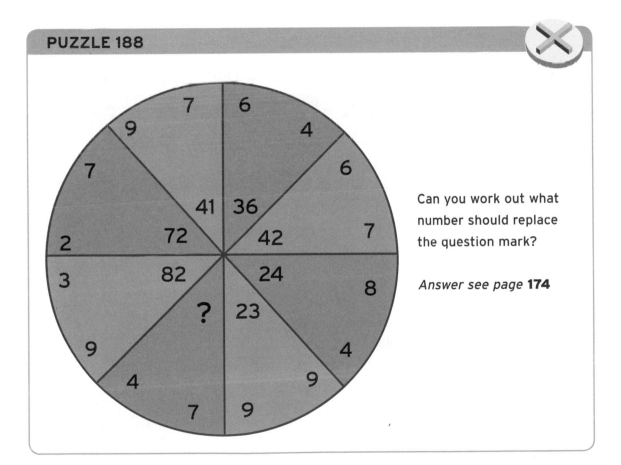

Can you work out what
number should replace
the question mark?

Answer see page **174**

PUZZLE 189

Five cyclists are taking part in a race. The number of each rider and its arrival time are in some way related. Can you work out the number of the rider who arrives at 2:30?

No. 10
Arrives 2:15

No. 2
Arrives 3:02

No. 30
Arrives 2:45

No. 8
Arrives 3:08

No. ?
Arrives 2:30

Answer see page **1674**

PUZZLE 190

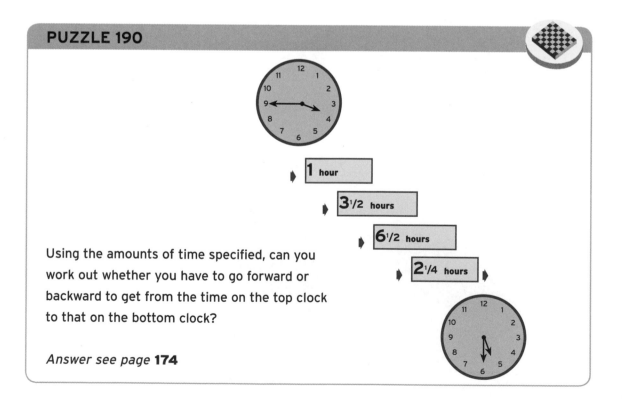

Using the amounts of time specified, can you work out whether you have to go forward or backward to get from the time on the top clock to that on the bottom clock?

Answer see page **174**

PUZZLE 191

Can you work out the reasoning behind this square and replace the question mark with a number?

Answer see page **174**

5	3	8	7
12	15	49	56
3	9	4	12
18	27	36	?

PUZZLE 192

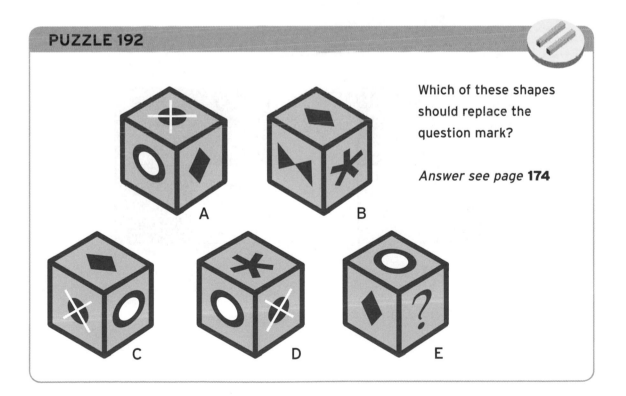

Which of these shapes should replace the question mark?

Answer see page **174**

What colour replaces the
question mark?

Answer see page **174**

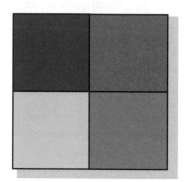

23

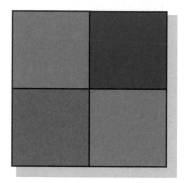

19

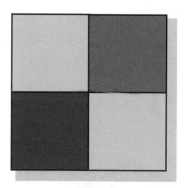

27

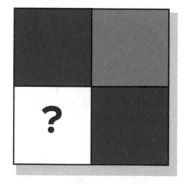

18

PUZZLE 194

Can you work out which of these symbols follows the sequence above?

Answer see page **174**

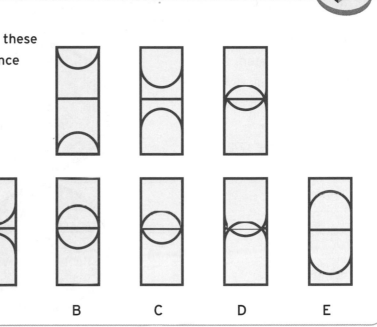

A   B   C   D   E

PUZZLE 195

Can you work out the reasoning behind these triangles and replace the question mark with a number?

Answer see page **174**

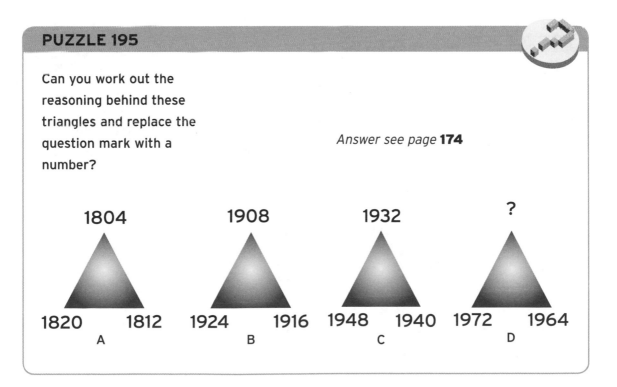

PUZZLE 196

The following clock faces are in some way related. Can you work out what the time on clock No. 3 should be?

Answer see page **174**

PUZZLE 197

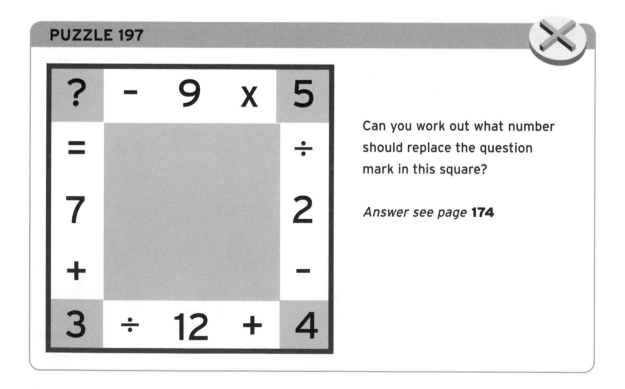

Can you work out what number should replace the question mark in this square?

Answer see page **174**

PUZZLE 198

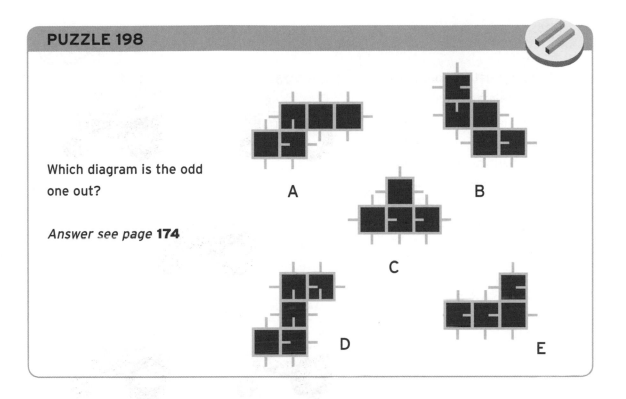

Which diagram is the odd one out?

Answer see page **174**

A

B

C

D

E

PUZZLE 199

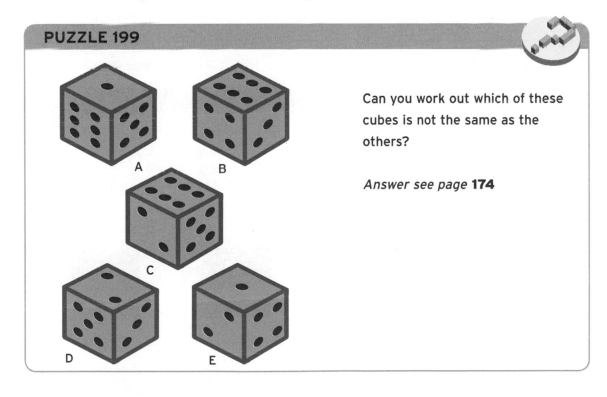

Can you work out which of these cubes is not the same as the others?

Answer see page **174**

A

B

C

D

E

PUZZLE 200

Each tractor gathers potatoes over a certain acreage (shown in brackets). The weight of potatoes in kilos is shown under each tractor. There is a relationship between the number of the tractor, the acreage and the weight gathered. What weight should tractor B show?

Answer see page **174**

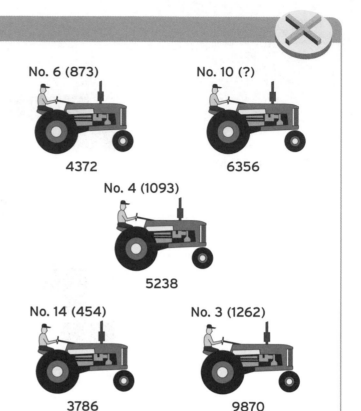

No. 6 (873)

4372

No. 10 (?)

6356

No. 4 (1093)

5238

No. 14 (454)

3786

No. 3 (1262)

9870

PUZZLE 201

Can you unravel the logic behind these squares and find the missing number?

Answer see page **174**

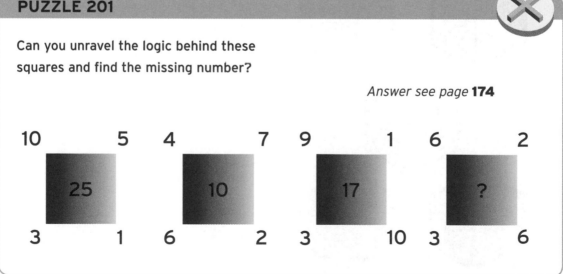

10　5　　4　7　　9　1　　6　2

25　　10　　17　　?

3　1　　6　2　　3　10　3　6

PUZZLE 202

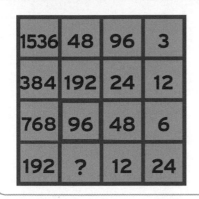

1536	48	96	3
384	192	24	12
768	96	48	6
192	?	12	24

Can you find the missing number in this square?

Answer see page **175**

PUZZLE 203

Can you work out what the next flower in this series should look like?

Answer see page **175**

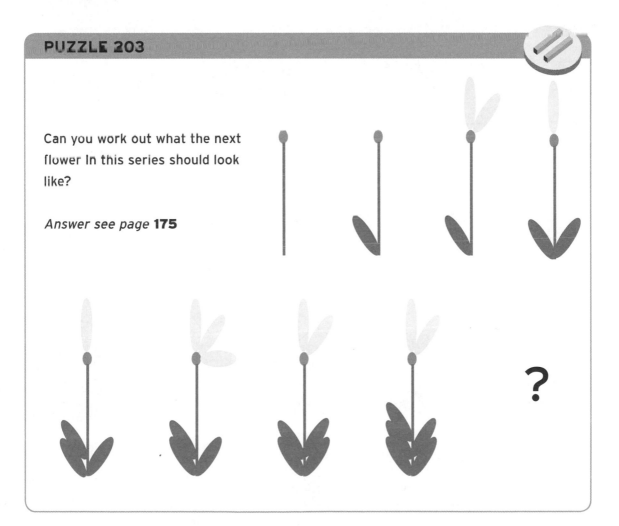

Medium
Answers

ANSWER 96

F. A curve turns into a straight line and a straight line into a curve.

ANSWER 97

C. It is the only one that does not have half as many 'step' lines as there are triangles.

ANSWER 98

2. The colors are worth Pink 1, Green 2, Orange 3, Yellow 4, Red 5, Purple 6. In each segment subtract the smaller outer number from the larger and put the difference in the center of the next segment clockwise.

ANSWER 99

- x + - ÷ +.
9 - 3 x 4 + 19 - 8 ÷ 5 + 4 = 11.

ANSWER 100

B. It is the only figure that, with an additional line, has a triangle adjoining the rectangle that overlaps the square.

ANSWER 101

7

ANSWER 102

E. A square becomes a circle, a circle a triangle, and a triangle a square of similar proportions and positions.

ANSWER 103

8. The sum of hands on each clock is 13.

ANSWER 104

It should have two dots. Add together the corner squares of each row or column and put the sum in the middle square of the opposite row or column.

ANSWER 105

The pattern sequence is:

Z R T T U W W Z Z S

Start at the bottom right and work up in a horizontal boustrophedon.

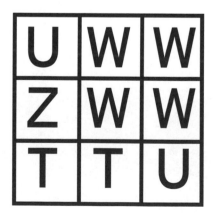

ANSWER 106

B. It is the only one with the same number of vertical and horizontal lines.

ANSWER 107

84. Multiply the hours of A by the minutes of B to get the tonnage of C, then B hours by C minutes to get D, C hours by D minutes to get E, D hours by E minutes to get A, and E hours by A minutes to get the tonnage of B.

ANSWER 108

G. The top and bottom elements swap position, the smaller central element becomes smaller still, and all three elements move inside the larger central shape.

ANSWER 109

E.

ANSWER 110

C.

ANSWER 111

B.

ANSWER 112

Spade = 2, Club = 4, Diamond = 6, Heart = 8.

ANSWER 113

The pattern is +1 lines, +2, +3, -2, -1, +1, +2, +3, etc. A figure with an even number of lines (ignoring the head) is turned upside down.

ANSWER 114

E. The shape has been folded along a horizontal line. A shaded piece covers an unshaded one.

ANSWER 115

D. Each column of elements alternates and moves up two rows.

ANSWER 116

6. The colors are worth Red 1, Orange 2, Green 3, Yellow 4, Pink 5, Purple 6, Brown 7. Add the outer numbers and put the sum in the center of the opposite segment.

ANSWER 117

D.

ANSWER 118

D. All the others are symmetrical.

ANSWER 119

12. Add together the values in the same segments in wheels A and C and put the answer in the opposite segment in wheel B.

ANSWER 120

C. It is the only one to have an odd number of one element.

ANSWER 121

D. Alternate between rotating the pattern 90° anti-clockwise, and swapping the direction of each individual arrow.

ANSWER 122

29. Add together the corner squares of each row or column in a clockwise direction. Put the sum in the middle of the next row or column.

ANSWER 123

The pattern sequence is: 1:00, 2:00, 2:00, 1:00, 3:00, 3:00, 2:00, 4:00, 4:00. 3:00, 5:00, 5:00, 4:00, 6:00, 6:00. Starting at the bottom left, work upwards in a vertical boustrophedon.

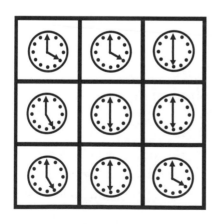

ANSWER 124

The pattern sequence is as follows.

 and spirals in a clockwise direction from the bottom left.

ANSWER 125

D. A circle becomes a square, a line a circle, and a square a line, all in the same size and position as the original.

ANSWER 126

Back, back, forward, back.

ANSWER 127

F. Circles and rectangles interchange except for strings of 3 circles, which disappear.

ANSWER 128

The faces pattern sequence is smiley, smiley, straight, sad, sad, smiley, straight, straight, sad, etc. Start at the bottom left and work in a horizontal boustrophedon.

ANSWER 129

23.

ANSWER 130

B. It consists of 14 straight lines, the rest of 13.

ANSWER 131

E.

ANSWER 132

B.

ANSWER 133

Yellow. The colors are worth Pink 2, Yellow 3, Orange 4, Green 5, Purple 6, Red 7, Brown 8. In each segment subtract the smaller of the outer numbers from the larger and put the result in the center of the next segment clockwise.

ANSWER 134

10. The colors are worth Orange 2, Red 3, Green 5, Yellow 6. The formula is 'add all three sides together'.

ANSWER 135

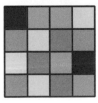

The colors are in the sequence Orange, Yellow, Pink, Red, Green and form an inward spiral starting at the top left.

ANSWER 136

The colors are worth Green 4, Purple 5, Red 6, Orange 8. The formula is left side plus base, minus right side.

ANSWER 137

6. The colors are worth Yellow 1, Green 3, Pink 4, Orange 5, Red 6, Purple 9. Add the outer numbers and put the result in the opposite segment.

ANSWER 138

G. Add 3 to odd numbers, subtract 2 from even numbers.

ANSWER 139

The pattern sequence is 7, 1, 1, 3, 2, 2, 5, 5, 4, 1. It starts at the top right and works in an anti-clockwise spiral.

4	2	2
1	5	5
7	1	1

ANSWER 140

A. Each shape increases by one of the same until there are three and it then becomes one. The image is reflected for a shape with two elements.

ANSWER 141

The pattern is +2 scales, +3 scales, -1 scale. A fish with an even number of scales faces the other way.

ANSWER 142

4.

ANSWER 143

B. The digits of all the others add up to 6.

ANSWER 144

A. Each ring contains one cross more than the previous example, and the first and last cross in each adjacent circle are level.

ANSWER 145

21. ← = 12, * = 9, ♥ = 3, % = 5, @ = 7.

ANSWER 146

D. The number of edges of the shapes in each square increases by 1 in each column, starting from the top.

ANSWER 147

14. Colors are worth Purple 2, Yellow 3, Orange 5, Green 6. Add sides together and put sum in center of triangle.

ANSWER 148

16.

ANSWER 149

14. The colors are worth Red 5, Yellow 3, Green 6, Blue 4. Add the sides together and swap the results within horizontally adjacent triangles.

ANSWER 150

D.

ANSWER 151

11. The colors are worth Brown 1, Green 2, Orange 3, Yellow 4, Pink 5, Red 6, Purple 7. Add the outer numbers in each segment and place in the center of the next segment clockwise.

ANSWER 152

3. The numbers rotate anti-clockwise from one square to the next and decrease by 2 each time.

ANSWER 153

9. Multiply the values in the same segments in wheels 2 and 3 and put the answer in the next segment in wheel 1, going clockwise.

ANSWER 154

Add the number of segments in column 1 to the number of segments in column 3. Draw this number of segments into column 2.

ANSWER 155

15. Take the number of minutes in the hours, add the minutes and divide by 10. Ignore the remainder.

ANSWER 156

E. Add two circles and two lines, take away one of each, repeat. The pattern is also rotated by 90° anti-clockwise each time.

ANSWER 157

27. Add all the numbers for each square. For Yellow add 5, for Green subtract 5. Then swap the numbers in adjacent Yellow and Green squares.

ANSWER 158

C.

ANSWER 159

21. Multiply each number by the number on the opposite side of the wheel on the same side of the spoke and put the product in that segment next to the center.

ANSWER 160

F. The circles and squares become squares and circles, respectively. The largest element loses all internal elements.

ANSWER 161

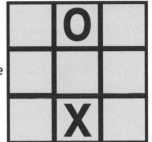

Starting at opposite ends the symbols move alternately 1 and 2 steps to the other end of the grid in a boustrophedon.

ANSWER 162

A.

ANSWER 163

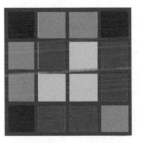

The sequence is Brown, Orange, Yellow, Brown, Purple, Green. It forms a diagonal boustrophedon (or ox plough pattern) starting in the bottom left corner.

ANSWER 164

The pattern sequence is 1, 2, 2, 3, 4, 4, 1, 2, 3, 3, 4. Start at the top left and work in a horizontal boustrophedon.

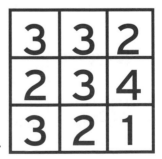

ANSWER 165

D. Add consecutive clockwise corners of the diamond and place the sum on the corresponding second corner. Add the four numbers together and place the sum in the middle.

ANSWER 166

No. 2. Take the first digit of the weight from the second to arrive at new number.

ANSWER 167

B. Each time the square becomes the circle, the triangle the square, and the circle the triangle.

ANSWER 168

92. Multiply the numbers on the diagonally opposite corners of each square and add the products. Put the sum in the third square along.

ANSWER 169

3:13. Start time A minus Finish A equals Finish B. Start time B minus Finish B equals Finish C, etc.

ANSWER 170

D. It is the only one to which a circle can be added where the triangle overlaps the circle and a right-angled line runs parallel to the whole of one side of the triangle.

ANSWER 171

C. Each row and column must contain two Orange and two Green squares.

ANSWER 172

B.

ANSWER 173

3.

ANSWER 174

J. All of the others have a matching partner.

ANSWER 175

E. All elements consist of 3 straight lines except 'E', which consists of 4 straight lines.

ANSWER 176

The pattern sequence is @, @, %, *, %, &, &, *, %. It starts at the top right and works inwards in an anti-clockwise spiral.

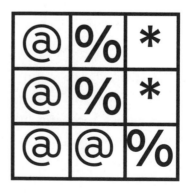

ANSWER 177

2.

ANSWER 178

44. The numbers increase clockwise first missing one spoke, then two at the fourth step. Each circle increases by a different amount
(2, 3, 4).

ANSWER 179

B.

ANSWER 180

B. The others all have an equal number of straight lines and curves.

ANSWER 181

The corresponding sections in each wheel should contain a black section in each compartment.

ANSWER 182

Starting with a vertical line reflect the dot first against that line and then each

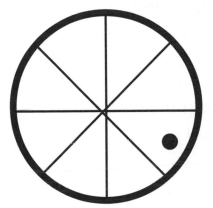

following line in a clockwise direction.

ANSWER 183

F. The small and large elements become large and small, respectively.

ANSWER 184

9. The numbers rotate clockwise and increase by 1 each time.

ANSWER 185

B. It is the only one to have an odd number of horizontal lines.

ANSWER 186

C. The number of small circles equals the number of edges of the shape,
except for 'C', where there is one more circle than edges.

ANSWER 187

10. Add 2 to each value, place sum in corresponding position in next triangle, then subtract 3, and add 2 again.

ANSWER 188

18. Multiply the numbers in the outer section, reverse the product and put it in the middle of the next section.

ANSWER 189

20. Multiply hours by minutes and divide by 3 to get the number of the rider.

ANSWER 190

Forward, back, forward, back.

ANSWER 191

48. In each box of four numbers, multiply the top two numbers, put the product in the bottom right box, then subtract the top right number from the bottom right one and put
the difference in the bottom left box.

ANSWER 192

ANSWER 193

Yellow (the numbers are added to give the totals).

ANSWER 194

B. Each arch moves closer to its opposite end by an equal amount each time.

ANSWER 195

1956. The numbers represent the leap years clockwise around the triangles starting at the apex. Miss one leap year each time.

ANSWER 196

9:05. The minute hand goes forward 25 minutes, the hour hand back by 5 hours.

ANSWER 197

13.

ANSWER 198

B. It is the only figure that does not have three boxes in one row.

ANSWER 199

C.

ANSWER 200

987. The tractor number is divided into the weight to give the acreage. The weights have been mixed up.

ANSWER 201

6. In each square, multiply the top and bottom left together, then multiply the top and bottom right. Subtract this

second product from the first and put
this number in the middle.

ANSWER 202

384. Starting at the top right-hand
corner work through the square in a
vertical boustrophedon, multiplying by 4
and dividing by 2 alternately.

ANSWER 203

Add one leaf. Add two petals.
Deduct 1 petal and add 1 leaf.
Repeat.

Hard Puzzles

Prepare to really feel your mind sweat! The puzzles in this section have all been carefully devised to push your mental functions to the absolute maximum. There are no easy solutions here, no quick gimmes – just lots and lots of really good, seriously challenging problems to test your capabilities. You'll need to use every trick you've learned to master the brain-benders in these pages – and you'll have to draw on some serious resolve and creativity, to boot.

But if the difficulty level of these problems is set to high, then so is the reward. The puzzles in this section are the ones that will really help you build new mental muscle. By stretching yourself beyond the point of everyday comfort, you are forced to strengthen and grow. That's as true of the mind as it is of the body. In a gym, these puzzles would be the final two or three extra-heavy lifts – the ones that do you as much good (or more) as all the workouts that went before them.

That's not all, either. These puzzles are a real challenge, and that means that solving them is a real achievement. As you work through the problems in this section, you'll feel the deep satisfaction of genuinely proving yourself against a serious obstacle. Every one you beat will become a badge of pride – another item to add to the stack of things you can feel good about. And that's every bit as important as the really great mental exercise you'll be doing. Play on: mind fitness awaits!

PUZZLE 204

Can you work out what the missing symbol should look like?

Answer see page 246

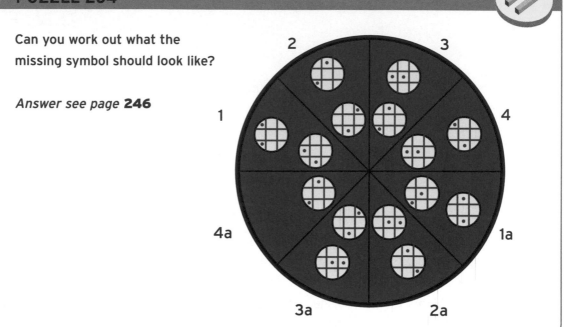

PUZZLE 205

Can you work out which symbol follows the series?

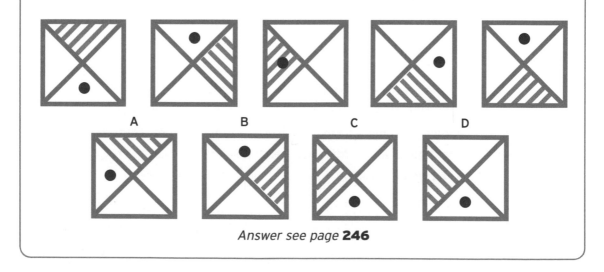

Answer see page 246

Can you work out the reasoning behind this grid and complete the missing section?

Answer see page **246**

PUZZLE 207

Can you find the number that should replace the question mark?

Answer see page **246**

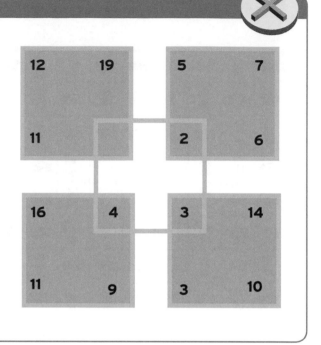

PUZZLE 208

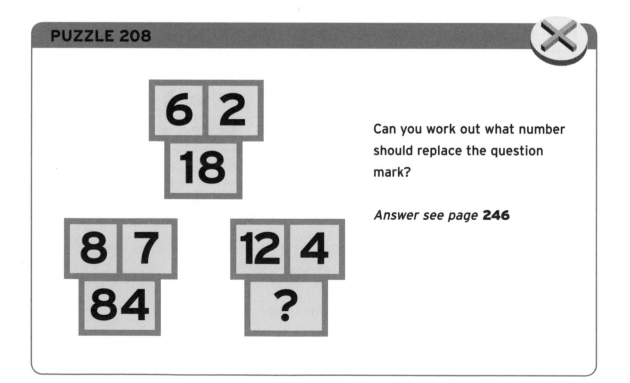

Can you work out what number should replace the question mark?

Answer see page **246**

Which two of these butterflies are identical?

Answer see page **242**

A

B

C

D

E

F

A   B

Can you find the
odd one out?

*Answer see
page 246*

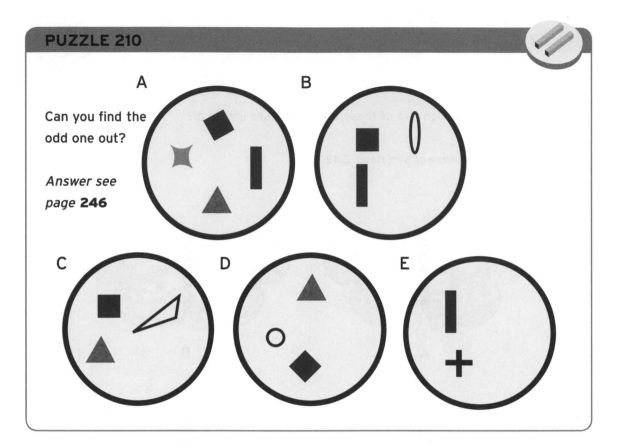

C   D   E

Can you unravel the reasoning behind this
grid and complete the missing square?

Answer see page 246

		2	7	3	8	4	9		2	7	3	8	4	9
9	9								2	7	3	8	4	9
4	4	3	8	4	9									
8	8	7			2	7	3	8	4	9				
3	3	2		4	9									
7	7			8	7	3	8	4	9			2		
2	2			3	2							7		
				7								3		
				2								8	2	
												4	7	
9												9	3	
4													8	
8				9	4	8	3	7	2				4	
3				9	4	8	3	7	2				9	
7		9	4	8	3	7	2							
2				9	4	8	3	7	2					

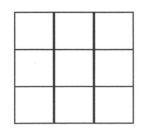

The numbers in this grid occur in the following order: 9, 4, 8, 3, 7, 2 and run in an anti-clockwise spiral starting at the top right. It is complicated by the addition of spaces and repeats according to a pattern.

Can you complete the missing section?

Answer see page **247**

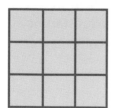

Can you work out the reasoning behind this grid and complete the missing section?

*Answer see page **247***

Which of the following is the odd one out?

Answer see page **247**

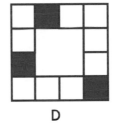

A   B

C   D

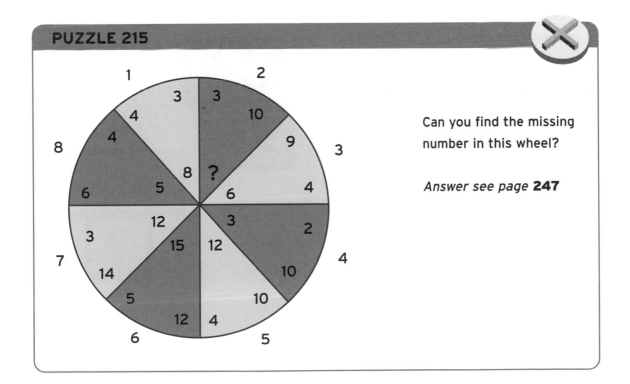

Can you find the missing number in this wheel?

Answer see page **247**

PUZZLE 216

Can you work out what the missing number is?

Answer see page **247**

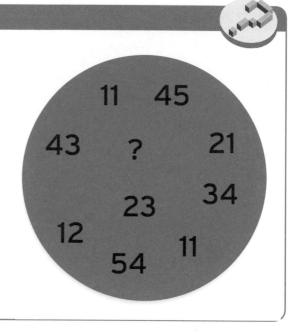

PUZZLE 217

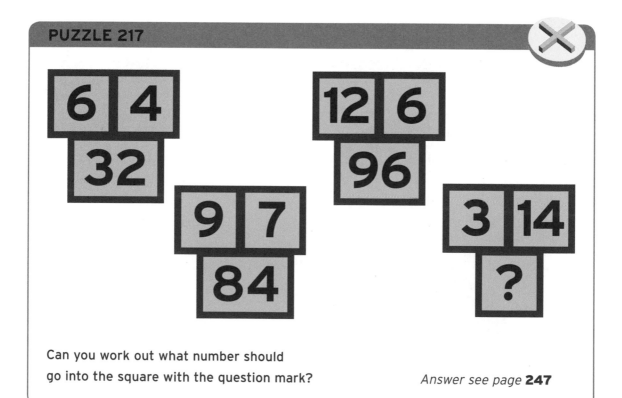

Can you work out what number should
go into the square with the question mark?

Answer see page **247**

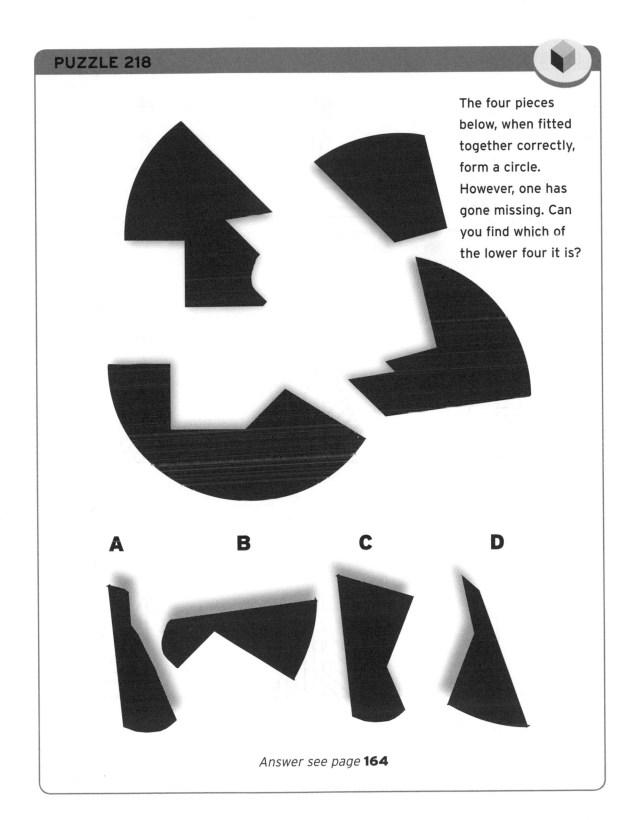

The four pieces below, when fitted together correctly, form a circle. However, one has gone missing. Can you find which of the lower four it is?

A   B   C   D

Answer see page **164**

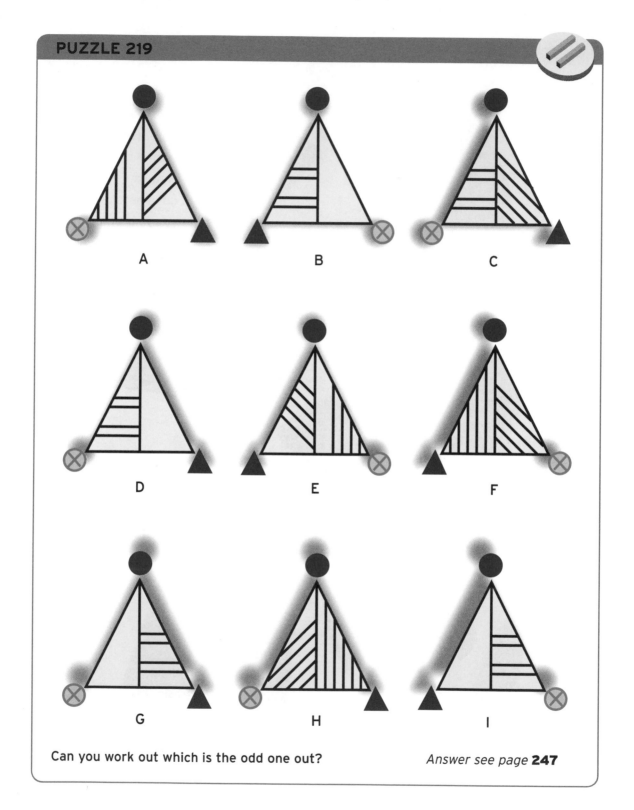

A

B

C

D

E

F

G

H

I

Can you work out which is the odd one out?

Answer see page **247**

Can you work out the reasoning behind this wheel and fill in the missing number?

Answer see page **247**

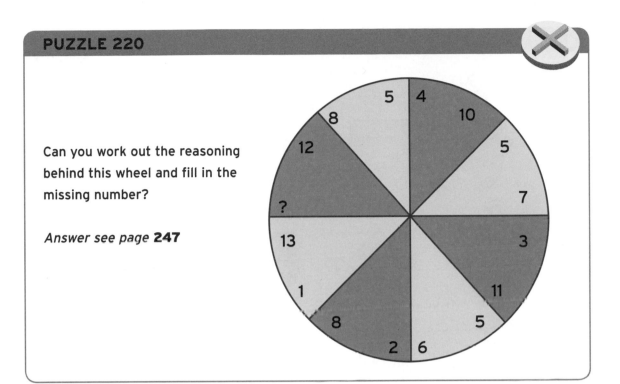

3	6	3	5
4	12	11	1
3	?	15	5
1	6	7	2

Can you unravel the reasoning behind this square and replace the question mark with a number?

Answer see page **247**

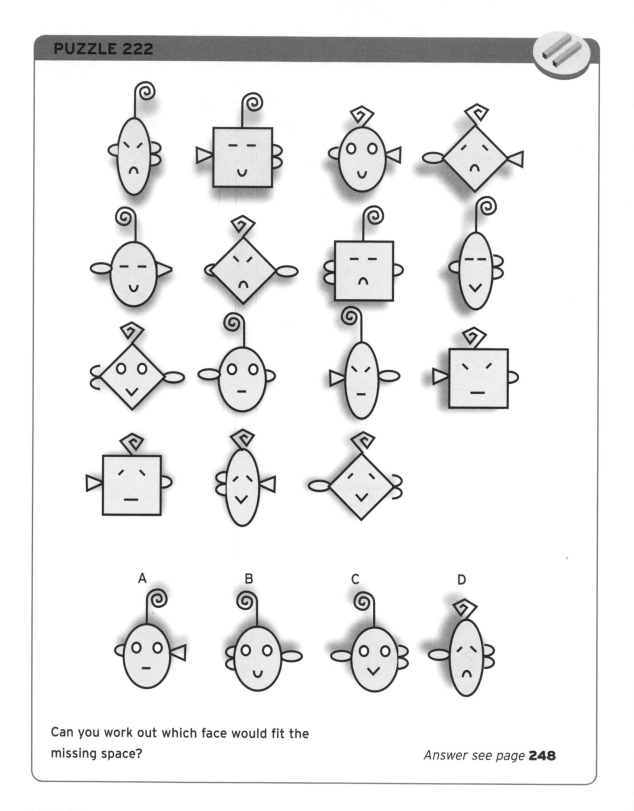

Can you work out which face would fit the missing space?

Answer see page 248

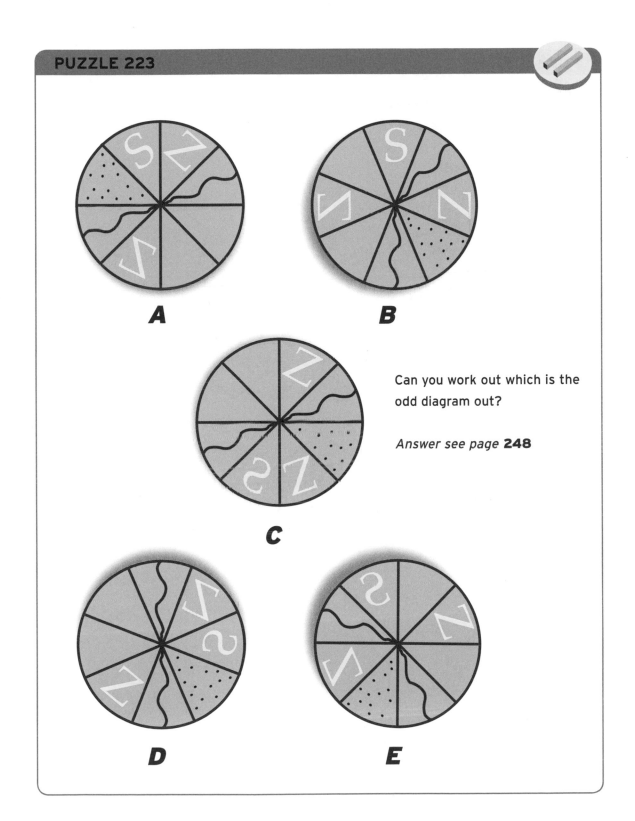

Can you work out which is the odd diagram out?

Answer see page **248**

Can you work out which two models cannot
be made from the above layout?

Answer see page **248**

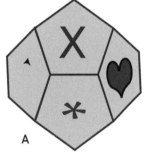

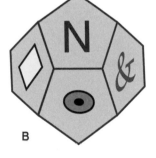

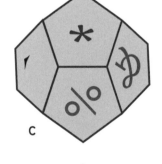

A

B

C

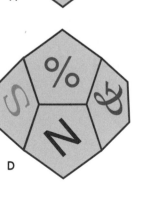

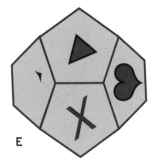

D

E

F

PUZZLE 225

Find a number that could
replace the question mark.
Each color represents a number
under 10.

Answer see page **248**

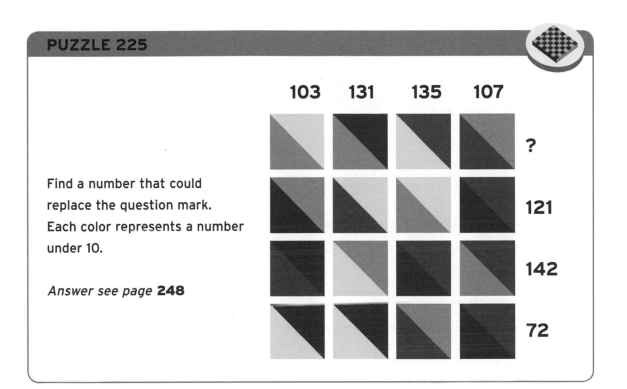

PUZZLE 226

Find a number that could
replace the question mark.

Answer see page **248**

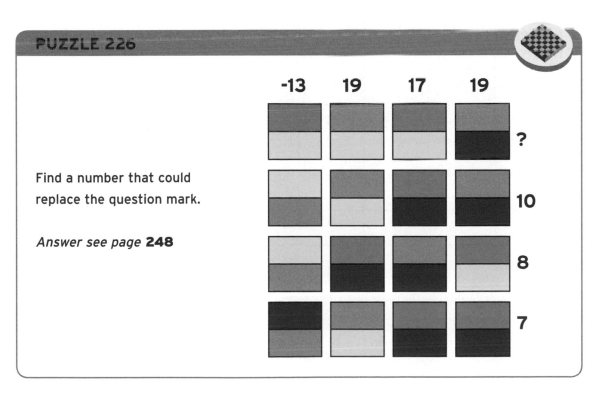

6	G	B	6	2	G	F	5
5	D	3	9	D	I	3	4
1	F	7	H	A	7	1	H
9	E	4	C	2	5	C	E
2	A	6	G	8	I	F	8
8	I	5			B	1	4
3	B	1			H	9	E
7	H	9	E	4	C	2	A
4	C	2	A	6	G	8	I
6	G	8	I	5	D	3	B
A	D	3	B	1	F	7	H
H	5	7	H	9	E	4	C
6	2	F	C	2	A	6	G
8	D	I	4	8	I	5	D
A	B	7	1	G	B	1	F
F	5	9	C	E	3	9	E

This grid follows the pattern: 5, 6, 4, 7, 3, 8, 2, 9, 1, with the letters (in their positions in the alphabet) alternately replacing numbers. Can you fill the missing section?

Answer see page 248

PUZZLE 228

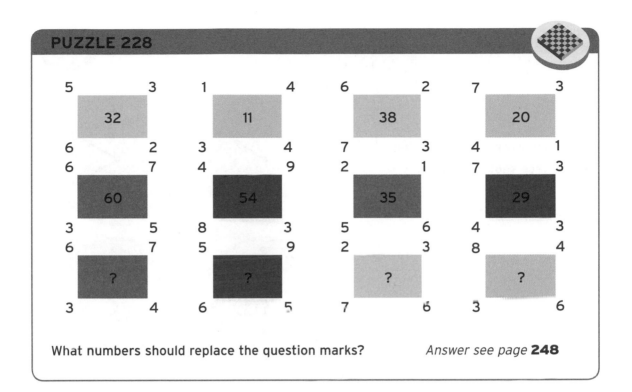

```
5          3     1          4     6          2     7          3
   [ 32 ]           [ 11 ]           [ 38 ]           [ 20 ]
6          2     3          4     7          3     4          1

6          7     4          9     2          1     7          3
   [ 60 ]           [ 54 ]           [ 35 ]           [ 29 ]
3          5     8          3     5          6     4          3

6          7     5          9     2          3     8          4
   [ ? ]            [ ? ]            [ ? ]            [ ? ]
3          4     6          5     7          6     3          6
```

What numbers should replace the question marks?

Answer see page **248**

PUZZLE 229

Find a number that could replace the question mark.

Answer see page **248**

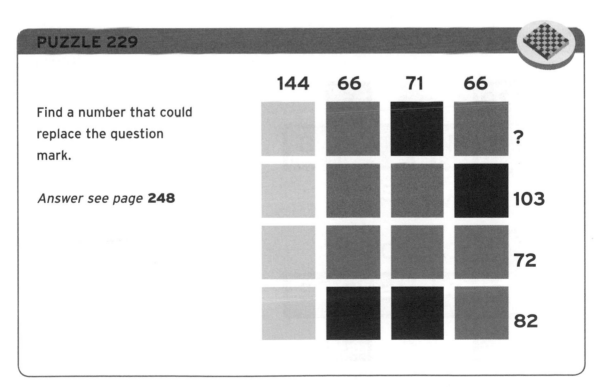

```
144    66    71    66
                        ?
                        103
                        72
                        82
```

PUZZLE 230

Can you work out what the last clockface should look like?

Answer see page **248**

PUZZLE 231

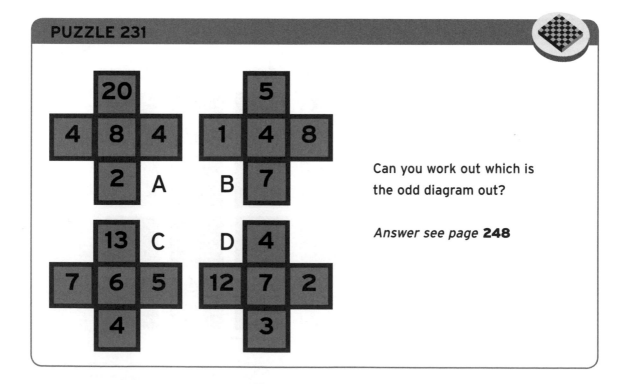

Can you work out which is the odd diagram out?

Answer see page **248**

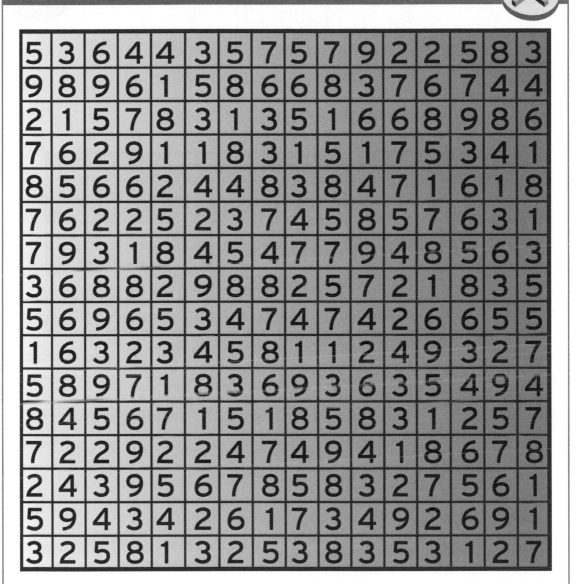

Look at this grid carefully and you will
find pairs of numbers that add up to 10,
in a either horizontal, vertical or diagonal
direction. How many can you spot?

Answer see page **249**

PUZZLE 233

How many yellow spotted tiles are missing from this design?

Answer see page **249**

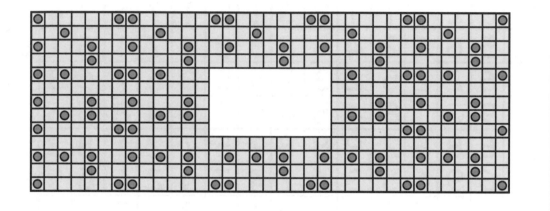

PUZZLE 234

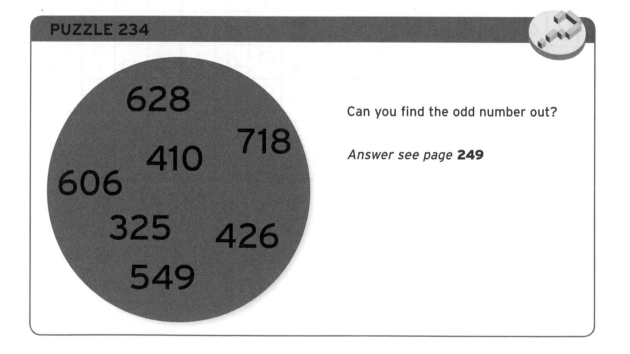

628

718

410

606

325

426

549

Can you find the odd number out?

Answer see page **249**

6	7	3	8	2	4	1	6	9	5	91
3	4	6	2	9	7	7	6	3	4	111
5	9	6	8	3	2	4	7			74
9	8	2	3			6	8			51
8	7	3	4			6	1	4	6	68
2	9	5	4	8	3	6	2	7	8	97
4	3	2	9	1	4	5	6	8	3	85
6	2	4	3	1	7	9	6	3	8	91
2	4	7	6			1	2			36
3	5	6	8			2	4			45

90 108 89 100 36 44 94 82 52 ?

Find a number that could replace the question mark. Each color represents a number under 10. Some may be negative numbers.

Answer see page 249

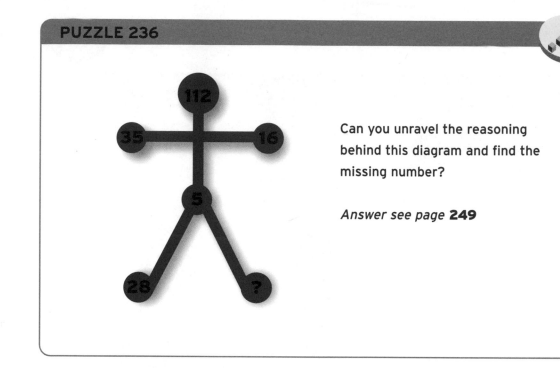

Can you unravel the reasoning behind this diagram and find the missing number?

Answer see page **249**

Can you work out what the square with the question mark should look like?

Answer see page **249**

3	4	6	9	7	2	5	8	3	9	?
6	5	2	7	3	4	5	1	2	6	71
3	8	2	1	9	7	8	6	1	3	82
5	4	3	4	1	2	9	8	6	5	85
6	8	9	3	5	4	8	3	6	2	91
4	1	9	8	6	3	2	2	4	5	74
7	6	3	5	2	4	6	8	9	7	93
8	4	6	5	3	6	2	1	3	8	83
9	2	1	4	3	7	8	9	6	3	88
1	3	7	6	4	3	8	6	2	4	77
89	75	77	87	79	86	81	93	67	102	

Find a number that could replace the question mark. Each color represents a number under 10.

Answer see page **249**

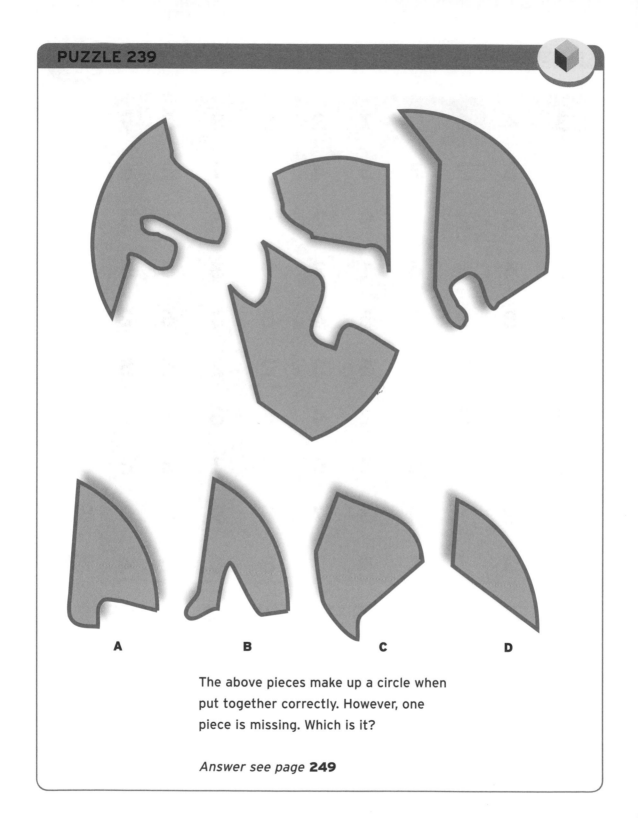

A

B

C

D

The above pieces make up a circle when put together correctly. However, one piece is missing. Which is it?

Answer see page 249

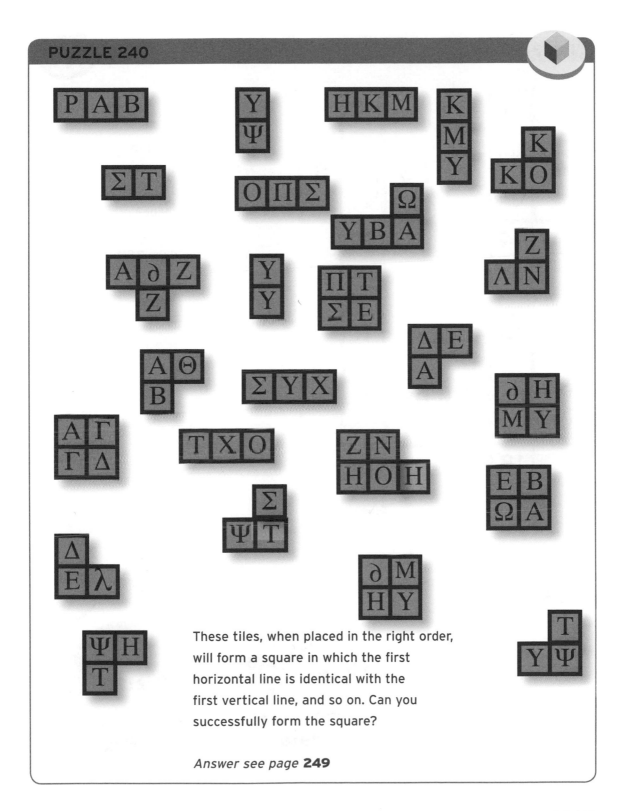

These tiles, when placed in the right order, will form a square in which the first horizontal line is identical with the first vertical line, and so on. Can you successfully form the square?

Answer see page 249

PUZZLE 241

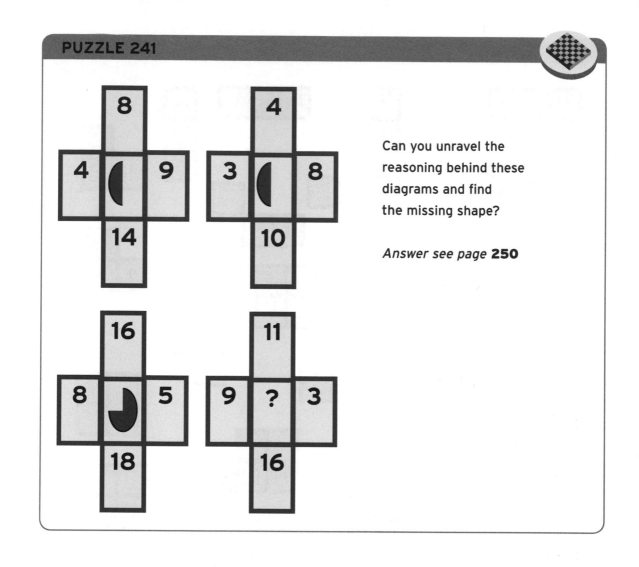

Can you unravel the reasoning behind these diagrams and find the missing shape?

Answer see page **250**

PUZZLE 242

Can you work out which is the odd number out in each circle?

Answer see page **250**

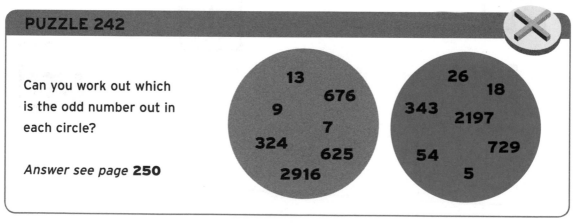

The above pieces, put together correctly, form a circle.
However, two extra pieces got mixed up with them which are
not part of the disc. Can you find them?

Answer see page **250**

Can you work out which diagram would follow the series above?

Answer see page **250**

A   B   C   D

PUZZLE 245

Can you find the missing number?

Answer see page **250**

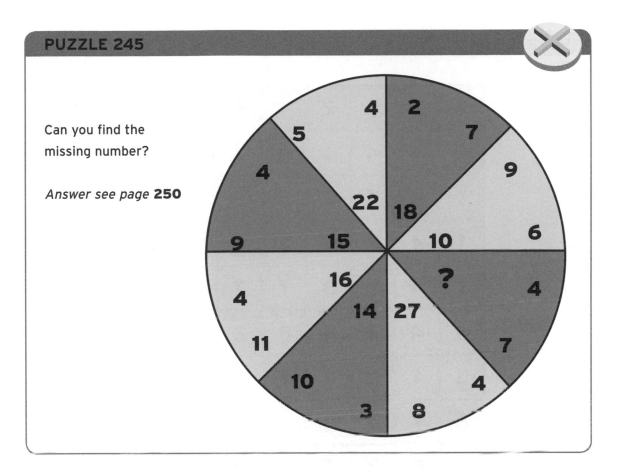

PUZZLE 246

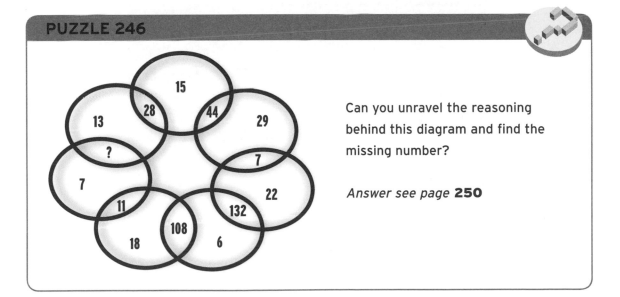

Can you unravel the reasoning behind this diagram and find the missing number?

Answer see page **250**

1	1	5	2	1	8	4	3
1	4	4	1	8	3	5	1
1	4	2	2	5	6	7	1
1	4	2	3	3	1	1	2
1	4	2	3	7	7	3	4
4	4	2	4	8	2	2	7
3	1	2	3	7	2	8	8
8	7	4	3	7	2	8	5
1	5	3	7	7	2	8	5
5	3	2	8	2	2	8	5
2	1	7	4	5	8	8	5
7	8	4	2	1	1	5	5

This grid follows the pattern: 3, 1, 4, 1, 5, 8, 2, 7. As a complication you will find some numbers have been increased by one. If you highlight these numbers you will discover a letter. What is it?

Answer see page **250**

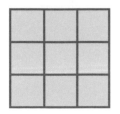

Can you work out the reasoning behind this grid and fill in the missing section?

Answer see page **250**

PUZZLE 249

Can you work out which shape should replace the question mark in this square?

Answer see page **250**

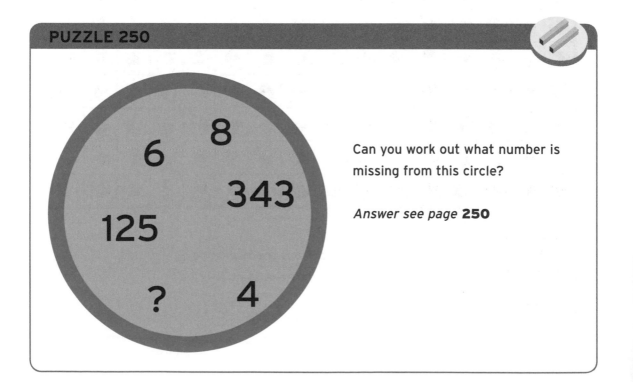

PUZZLE 250

Can you work out what number is missing from this circle?

Answer see page **250**

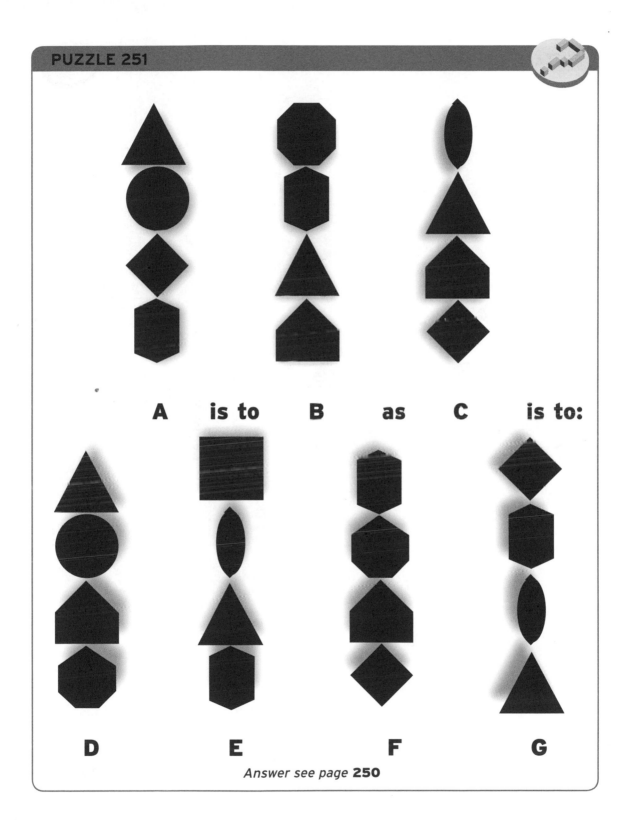

A is to B as C is to:

D E F G

Answer see page 250

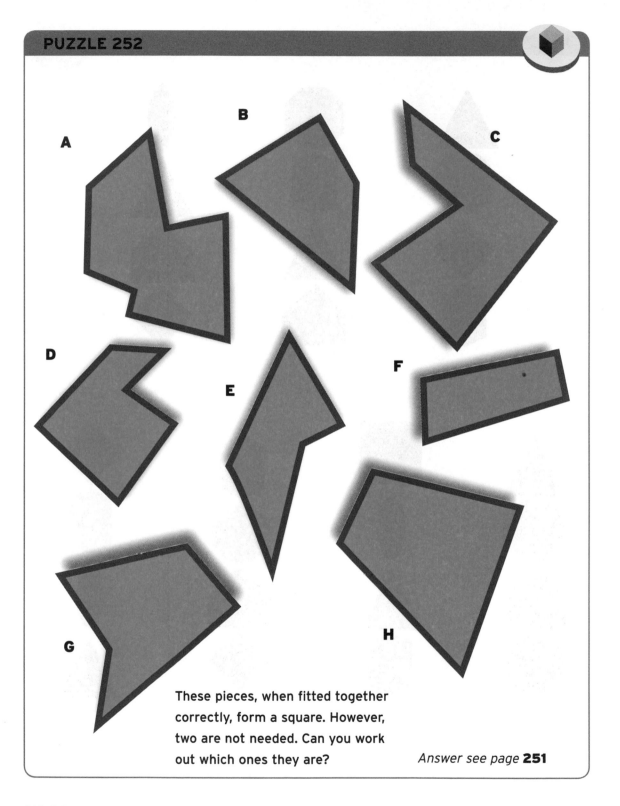

A

B

C

D

E

F

G

H

These pieces, when fitted together correctly, form a square. However, two are not needed. Can you work out which ones they are?

Answer see page **251**

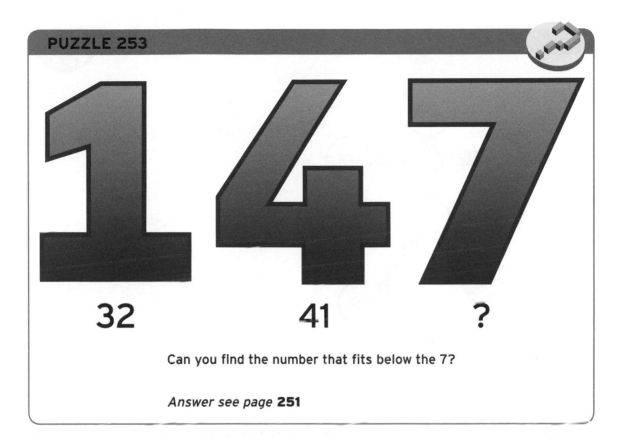

32   **41**   **?**

Can you find the number that fits below the 7?

*Answer see page **251***

Can you unravel the reasoning behind this wheel and replace the question mark with a number?

*Answer see page **251***

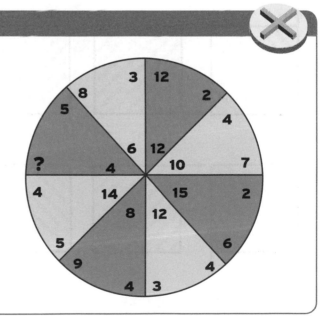

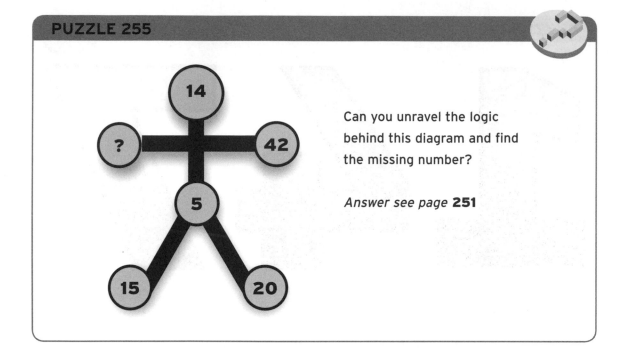

Can you unravel the logic behind this diagram and find the missing number?

*Answer see page **251***

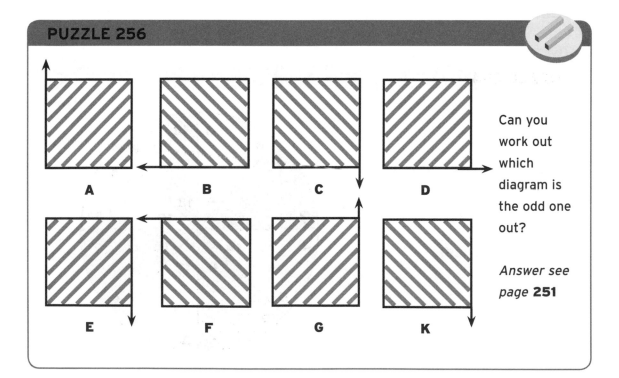

Can you work out which diagram is the odd one out?

*Answer see page **251***

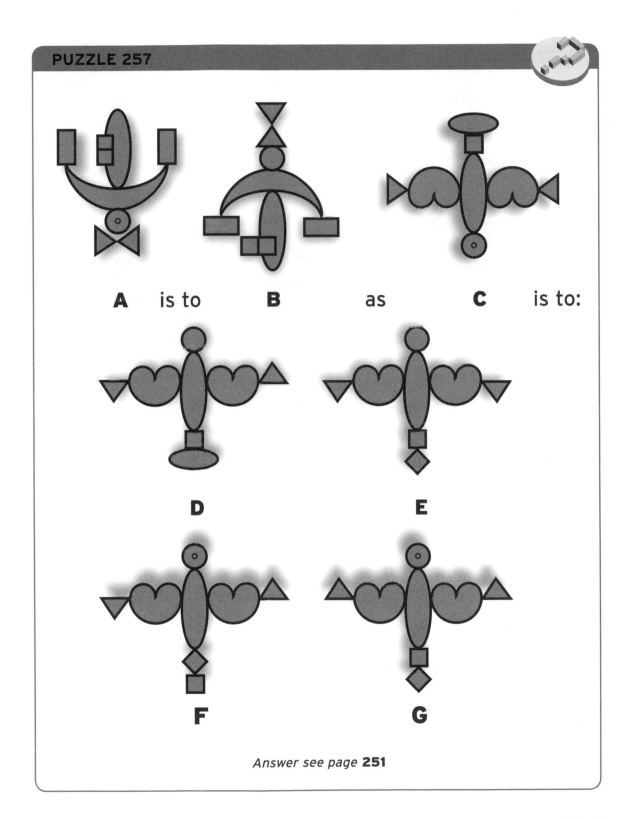

A is to B as C is to:

D

E

F

G

Answer see page 251

Can you work out which two models cannot
be made from the above layout?

Answer see page **251**

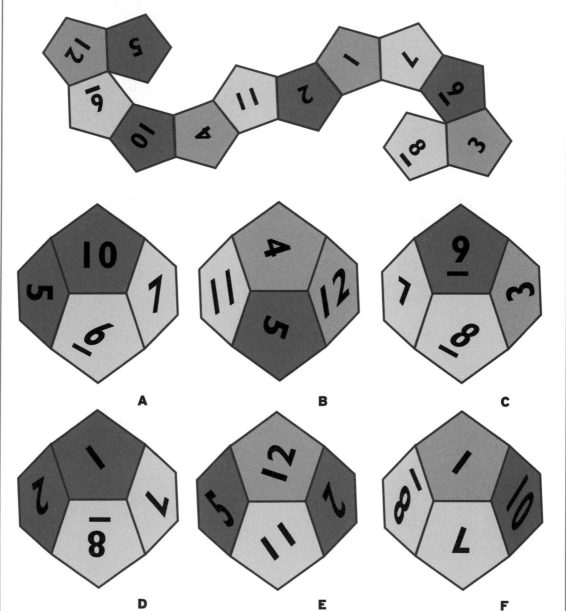

A

B

C

D

E

F

PUZZLE 259

These pieces, when fitted together correctly, make up a square.
However, one piece is not needed. Can you work out which one it is?

Answer see page **251**

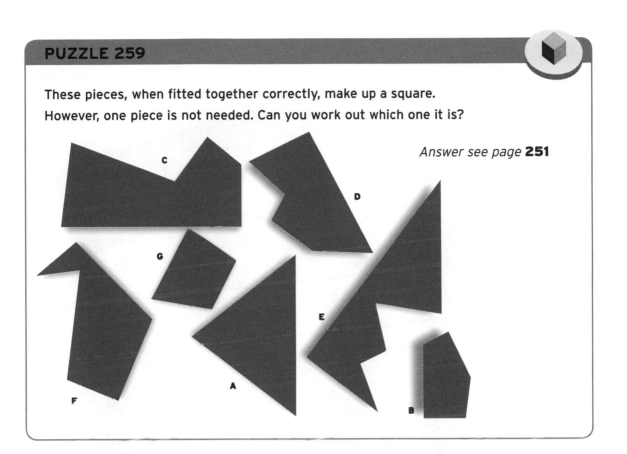

PUZZLE 260

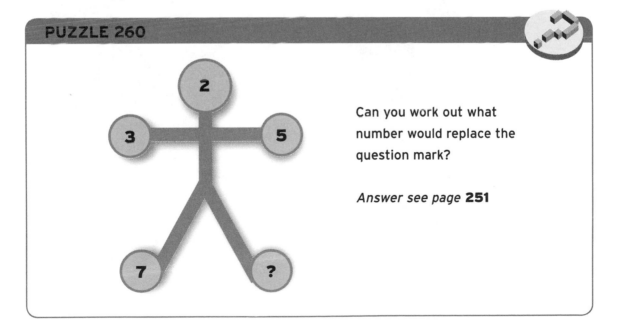

Can you work out what
number would replace the
question mark?

Answer see page **251**

The above pieces, when fitted together correctly, form a square. However, one wrong piece is among them. Can you work out which one it is?

Answer see page **251**

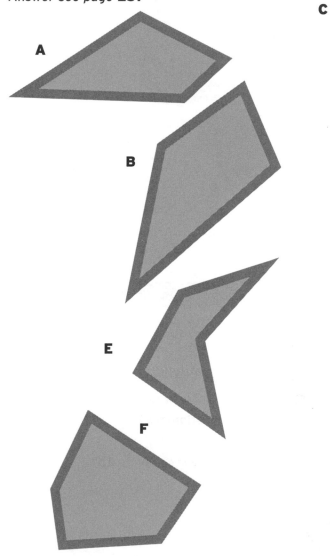

PUZZLE 262

Can you find the odd number out?

Answer see page **251**

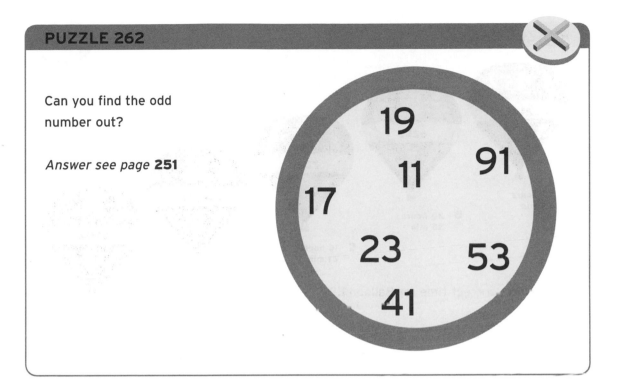

PUZZLE 263

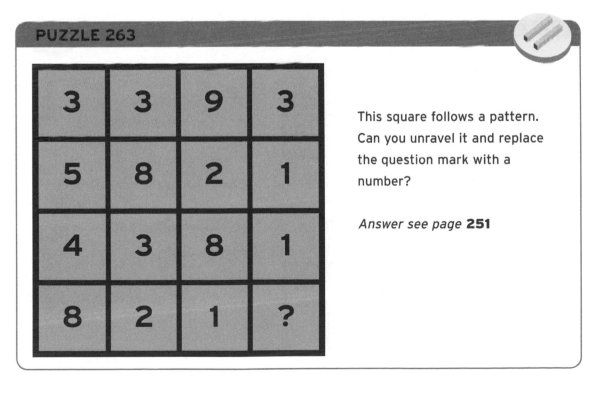

This square follows a pattern. Can you unravel it and replace the question mark with a number?

Answer see page **251**

PUZZLE 264

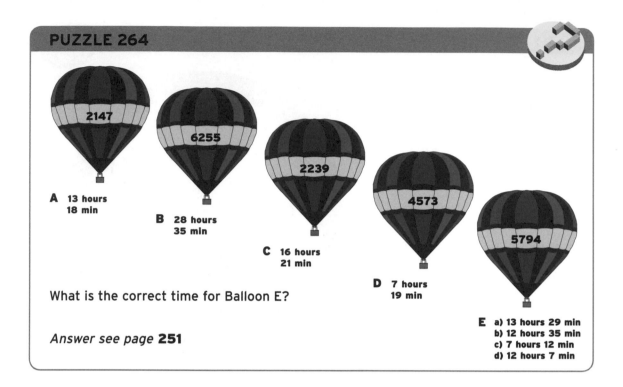

2147

6255

2239

4573

5794

A 13 hours 18 min

B 28 hours 35 min

C 16 hours 21 min

D 7 hours 19 min

E a) 13 hours 29 min
b) 12 hours 35 min
c) 7 hours 12 min
d) 12 hours 7 min

What is the correct time for Balloon E?

Answer see page **251**

PUZZLE 265

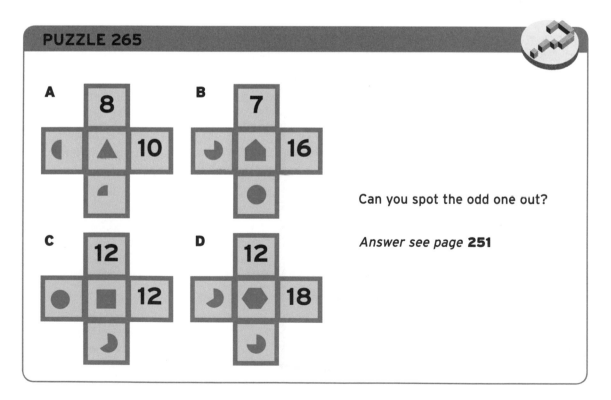

A

8

10

B

7

16

C

12

12

D

12

18

Can you spot the odd one out?

Answer see page **251**

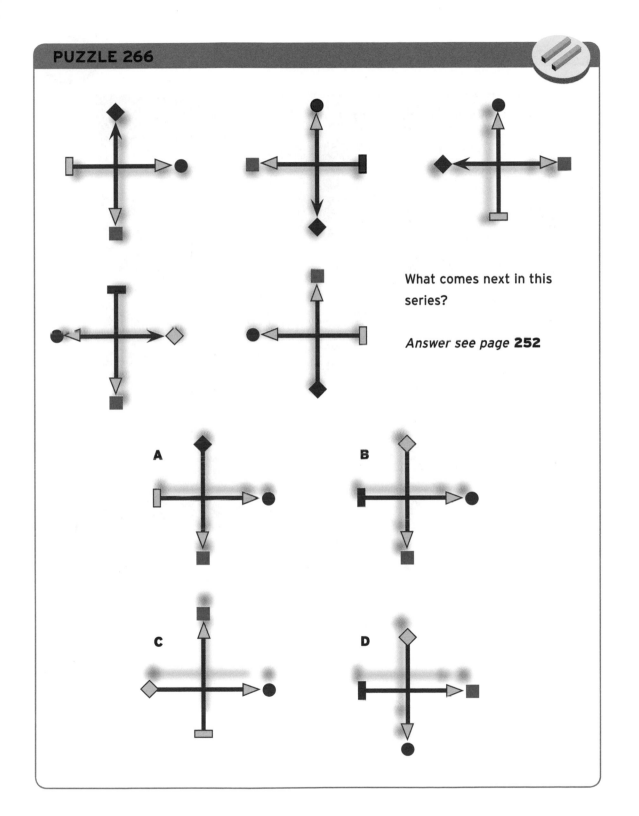

What comes next in this series?

Answer see page **252**

4	8	3	2	7	5	6	1	9	4	?
2	3	7	6	2	4	1	5	3	7	90
8	7	3	2	4	6	9	1	4	2	101
4	3	6	8	2	9	7	6	8	7	115
3	2	1	6	9	8	8	7	3	4	101
6	2	3	8	4	1	9	7	2	6	104
7	3	4	2	1	9	4	5	3	5	100
6	5	4	3	2	8	4	7	6	1	103
3	5	2	1	8	6	9	4	3	7	106
6	8	7	3	2	4	5	9	5	6	109

103 98 99 100 81 117 121 109 99 107

Find a number that could replace the question mark. Each color represents a number under 10.

Answer see page 252

PUZZLE 268

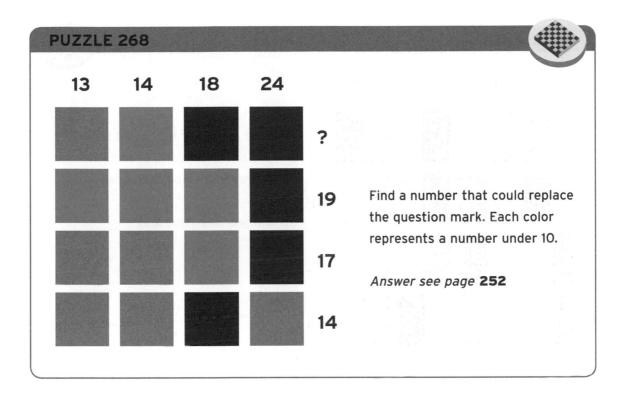

13 14 18 24

?

19

17

14

Find a number that could replace the question mark. Each color represents a number under 10.

Answer see page **252**

PUZZLE 269

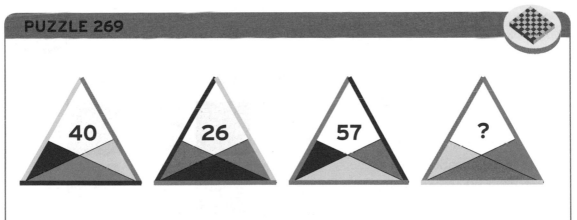

40   26   57   ?

Find a number that could replace the question mark. Each color represents a number under 10.

Answer see page **252**

PUZZLE 270

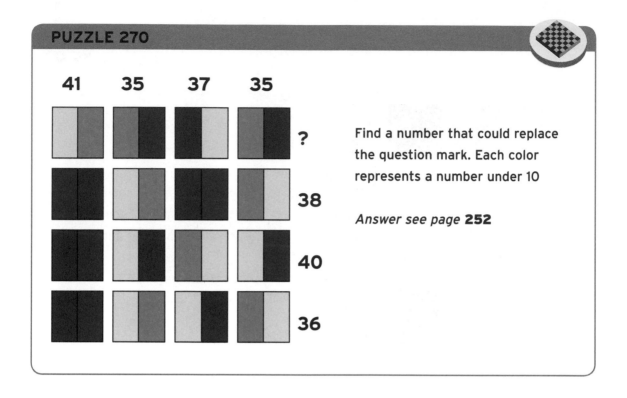

41   35   37   35

?

38

40

36

Find a number that could replace the question mark. Each color represents a number under 10

Answer see page **252**

PUZZLE 271

Find a number that could replace the question mark. Each color represents a number under 10.

Answer see page **252**

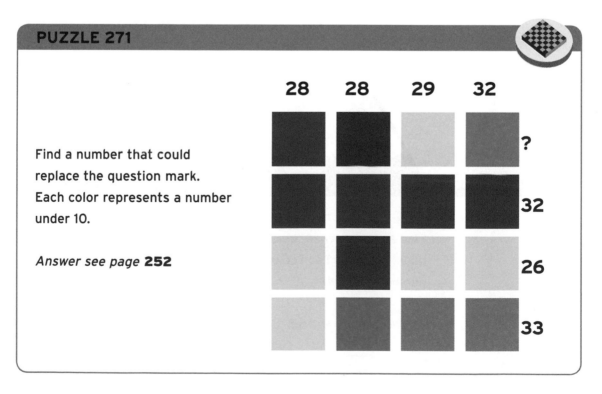

28   28   29   32

?

32

26

33

If the black arrow pulls in
the direction indicated,
will the load rise or fall?

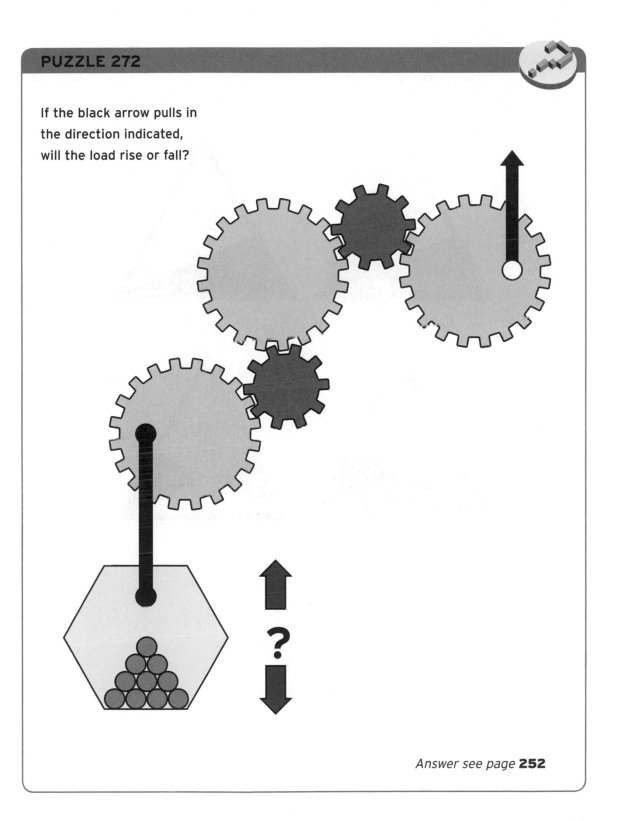

Answer see page **252**

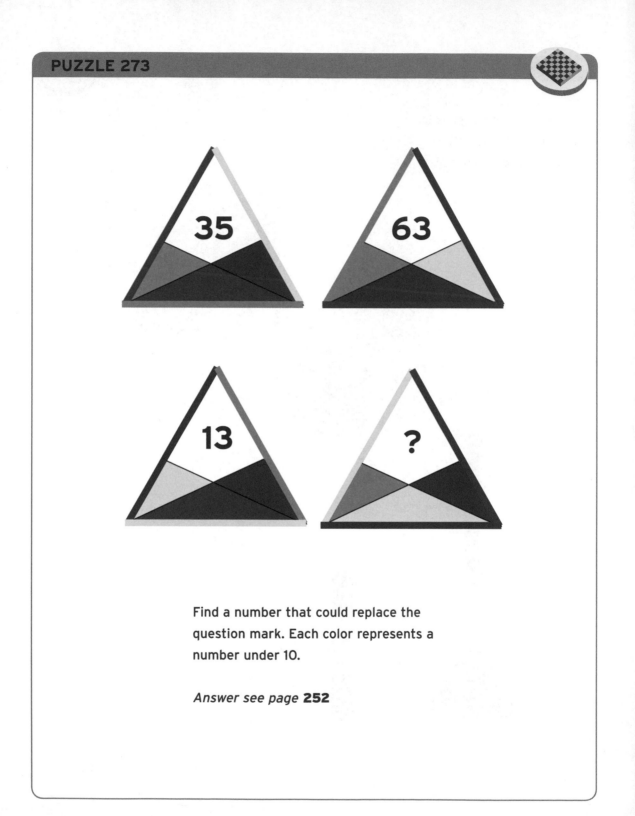

Find a number that could replace the question mark. Each color represents a number under 10.

Answer see page **252**

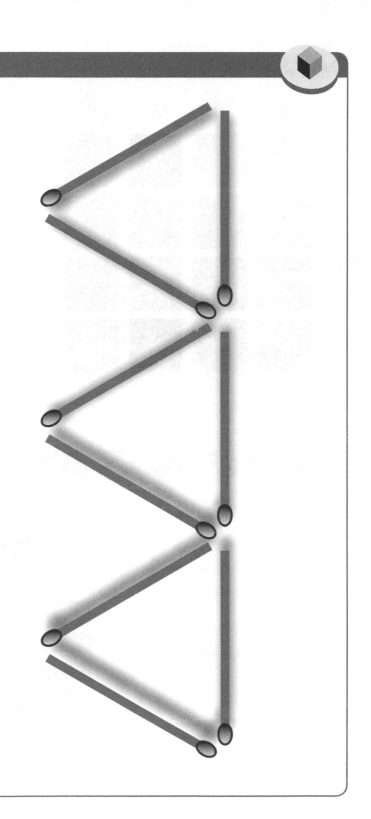

Take 9 matches or toothpicks and lay them out in 3 triangles. By moving 3 matches try to make 5 triangles.

Answer see page **252**

PUZZLE 275

13	14	18	24	

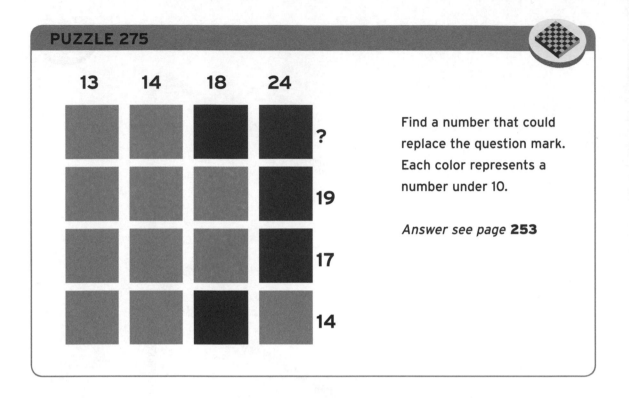

?
19
17
14

Find a number that could replace the question mark. Each color represents a number under 10.

Answer see page **253**

PUZZLE 276

Find a number that could replace the question mark. Each color represents a number under 10.

Answer see page **253**

35	28	34	34	

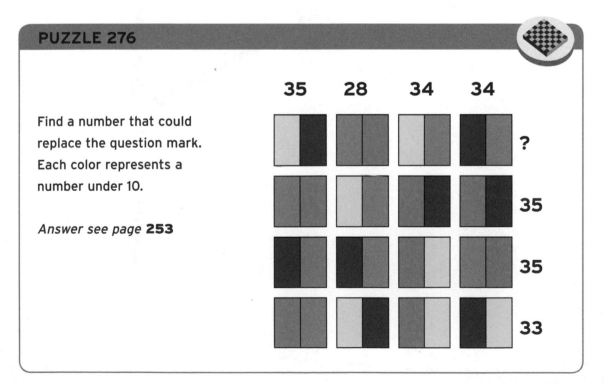

?
35
35
33

Have a look at the strange watches below. By cracking the logic that connects them you should be able to work out what time should be shown on the face of the fifth watch.

Answer see page **253**

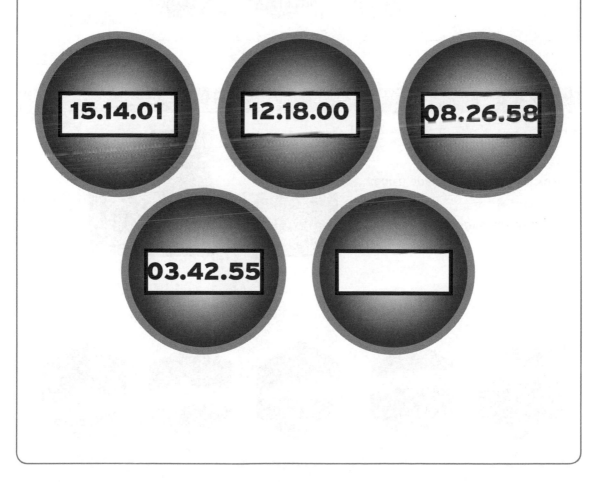

PUZZLE 278

Which of the following forms a perfect circle when combined with the diagram on the right?

Answer see page **253**

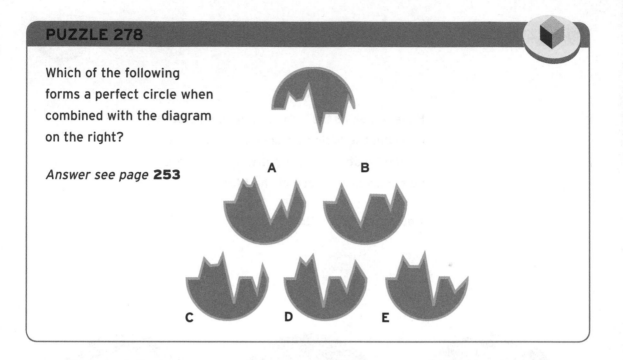

A B

C D E

PUZZLE 279

Which cube can be made using:

Answer see page **253**

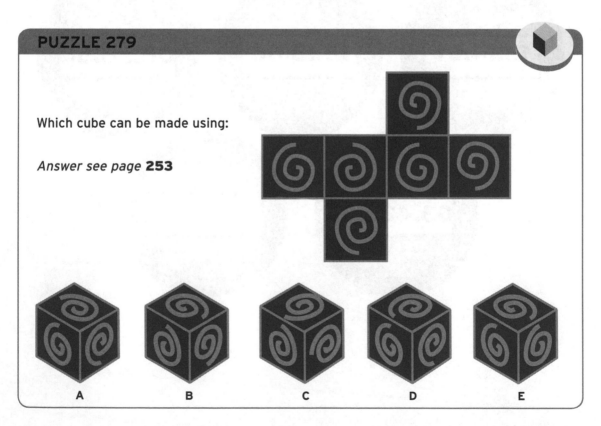

A B C D E

When old gardener Lincoln died, he left his grandchildren
19 rose bushes each. The grandchildren, Agnes (A), Billy
(B), Catriona (C) and Derek (D), hated each other, and
so decided to fence off their plots as shown. Who had to
build the greatest run of fence?

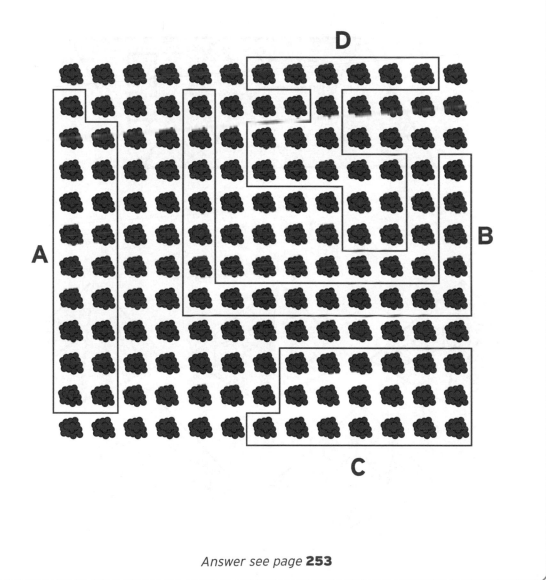

Answer see page **253**

Which of the following can be constructed
using this layout?

Answer see page **253**

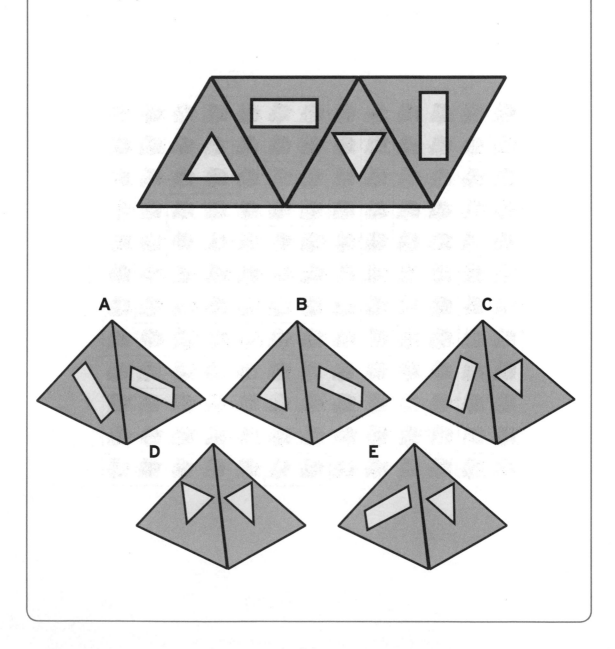

A

B

C

D

E

PUZZLE 282

Which is the odd one out?

Answer see page **253**

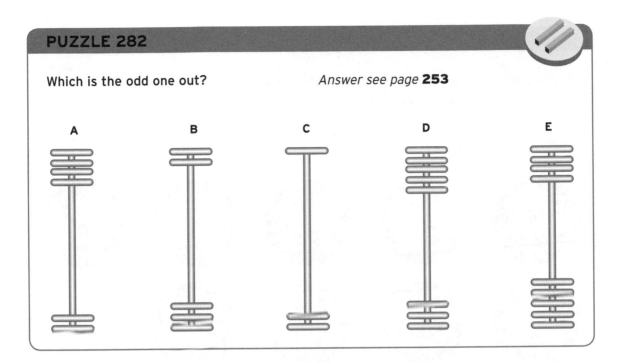

PUZZLE 283

What comes next in the sequence?

Answer see page **253**

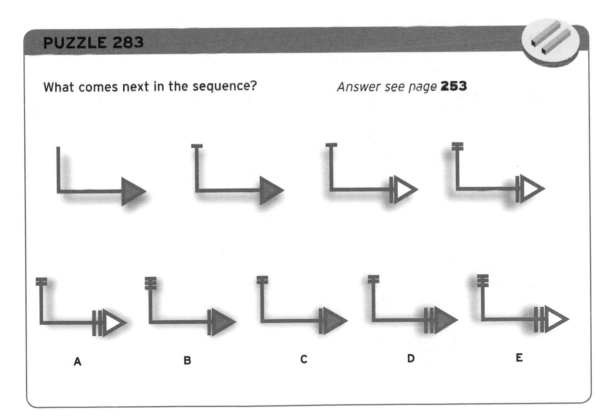

PUZZLE 284

Try to work out the fiendish logic behind this series of clocks and replace the question mark.

Answer see page **253**

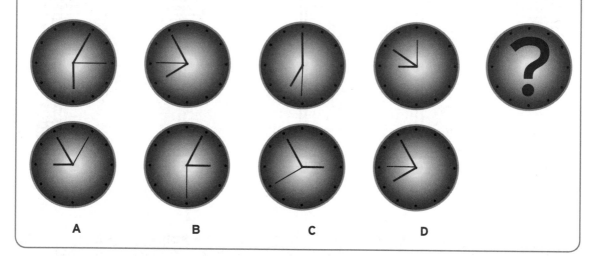

A   B   C   D

PUZZLE 285

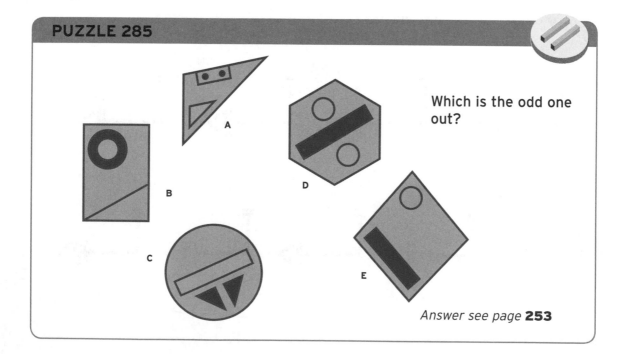

Which is the odd one out?

Answer see page **253**

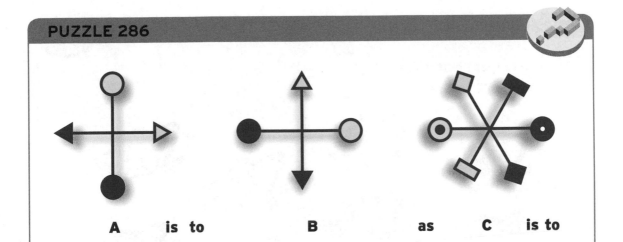

A   is to   B   as   C   is to

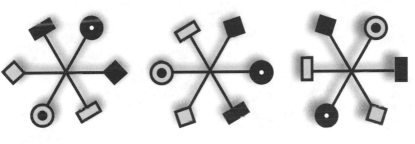

D   E   F

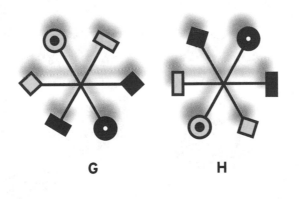

G   H

*Answer see page **253***

Only two of these butterflies
are identical. Which are they?

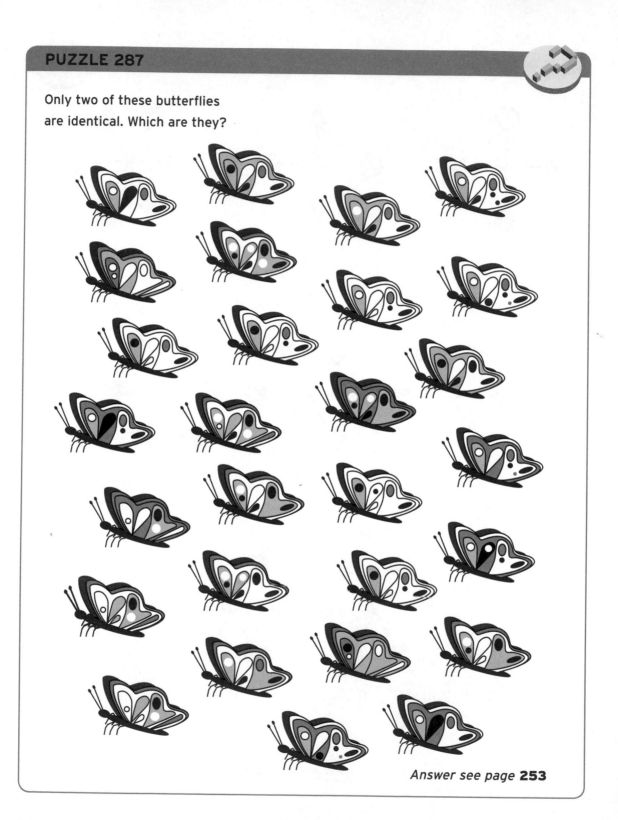

*Answer see page **253***

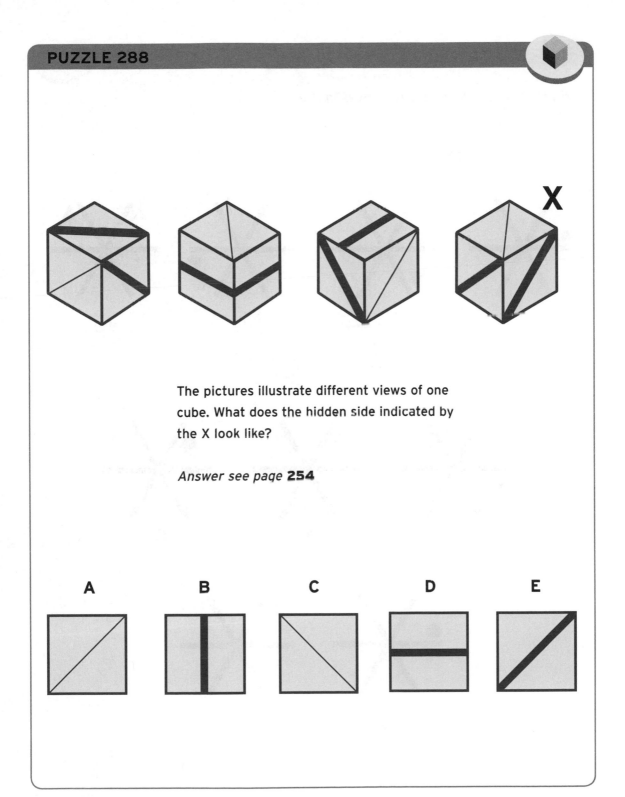

The pictures illustrate different views of one cube. What does the hidden side indicated by the X look like?

Answer see page **254**

A   B   C   D   E

Which of the following comes next in the
sequence?

Answer see page **254**

PUZZLE 290

The values of the segments are 3 consecutive numbers under 10. The yellow is worth 7 and the sum of the segments equals 50. What do the blue and green segments equal?

Answer see page **254**

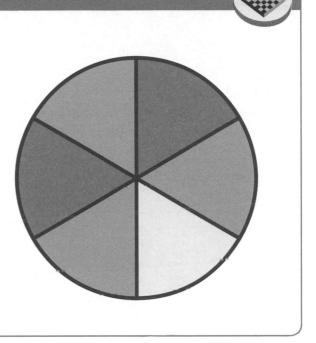

PUZZLE 291

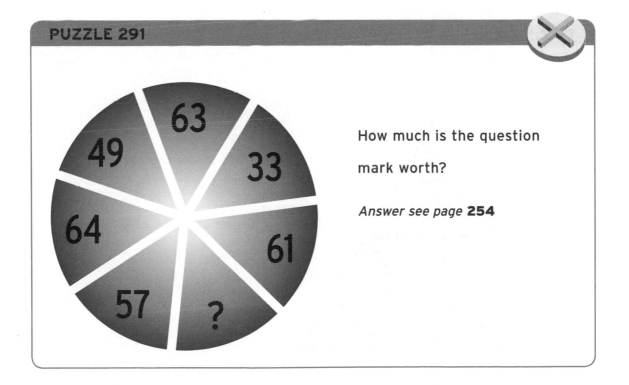

How much is the question mark worth?

Answer see page **254**

PUZZLE 292

Look at these triangles. What geometrical shape should logically be placed in the fourth triangle?

Answer see page **254**

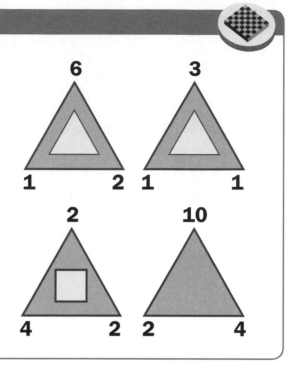

PUZZLE 293

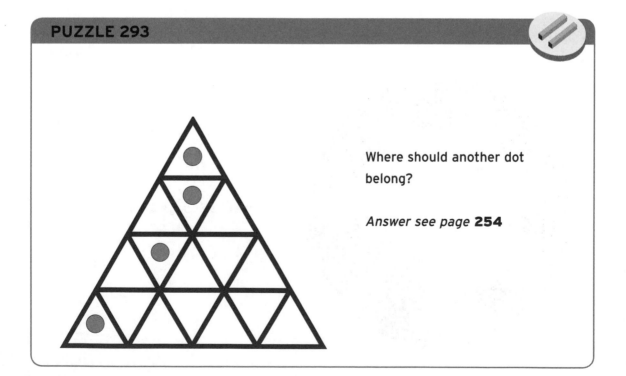

Where should another dot belong?

Answer see page **254**

PUZZLE 294

Which comes next in the sequence?

Answer see page **254**

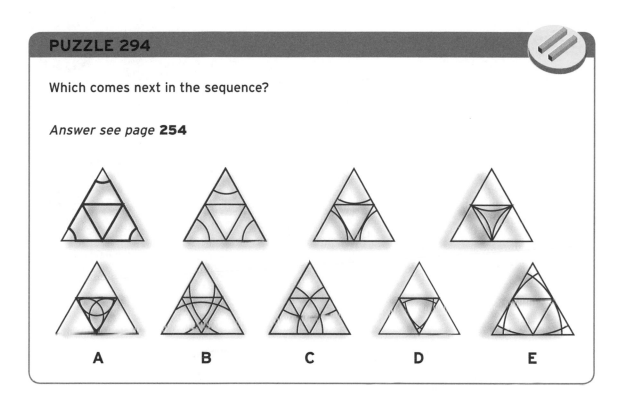

A B C D E

PUZZLE 295

Which is the odd one out?   *Answer see page* **254**

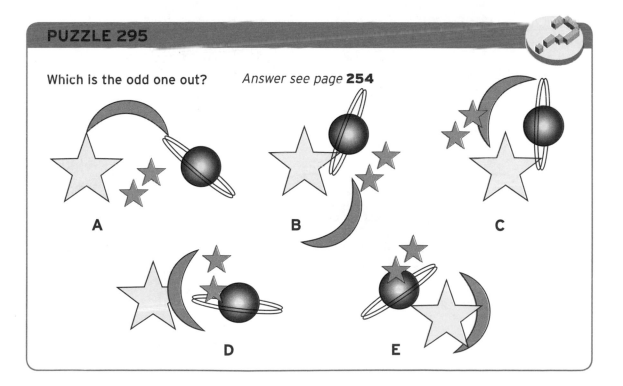

A B C

D E

PUZZLE 296

What comes next in the sequence?

Answer see page **254**

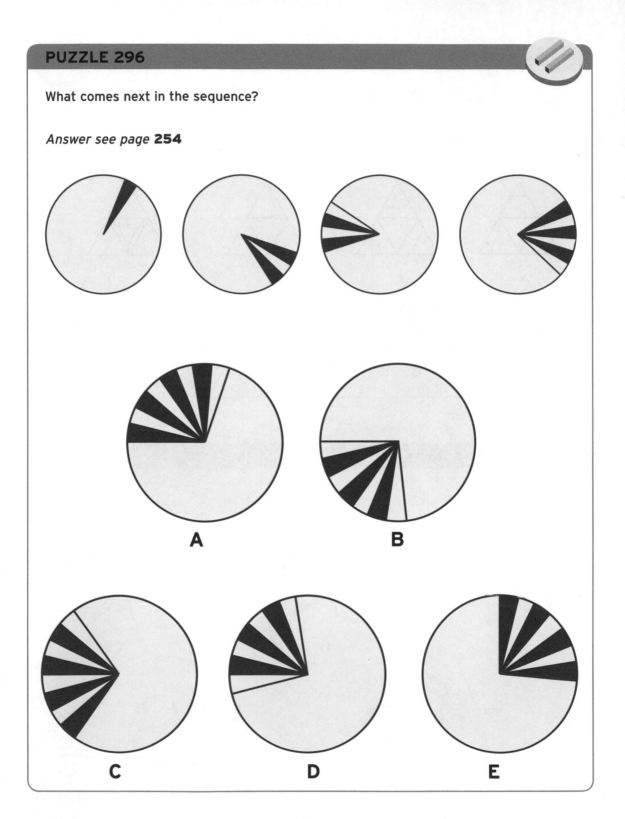

A

B

C

D

E

Answer see page **254**

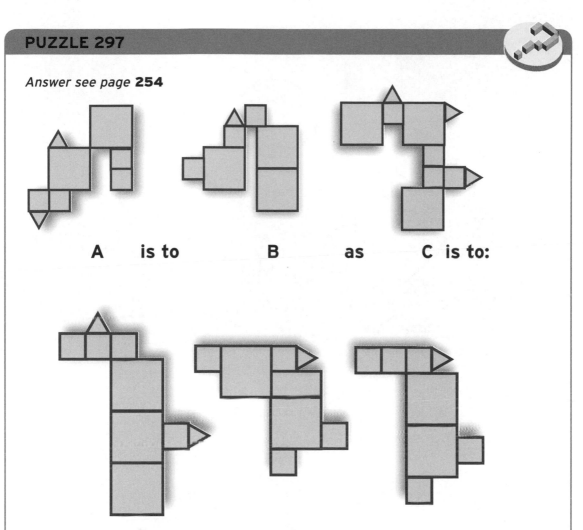

A   is to   B   as   C is to:

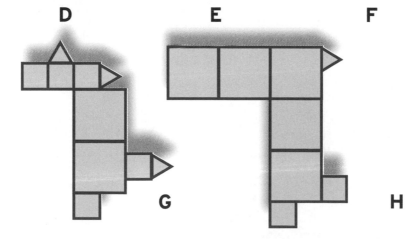

D

E

F

G

H

Hard
Answers

ANSWER 204

Reading across segments 1 and 1a, 2 and 2a, etc, the dots move around the circle in a vertical boustrophedon.

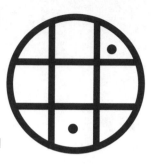

ANSWER 205

D. The striped section moves clockwise by 1, 2, 3 and 4 sections (repeat). Each time it moves by 2 and 4 sections the pattern is reflected. The dot moves 2 sections clockwise and 1 section anti-clockwise alternately.

ANSWER 206

The pattern sequence is shown below. Starting at the bottom right, work in a diagonal boustrophedon (clockwise start).

ANSWER 207

7. Add the three numbers on the outside of each square (A). Add the digits of the sum (B). Divide A by B and place in the small square.

ANSWER 208

72. Halve the number on the top left, multiply the number on the top right by 3. Multiply the two resulting numbers with each other, and put the product in the bottom square.

ANSWER 209

A and F.

ANSWER 210

C. It is the only circle with an asymmetrical shape.

ANSWER 211

The pattern is and the puzzle is a boustrophedon starting in the bottom right-hand corner.

ANSWER 212

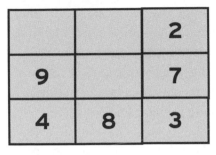

ANSWER 213

The pattern sequence is shown below. It starts at the top right and works down in a diagonal boustrophedon (anti-clockwise start).

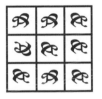

ANSWER 214

B. This is a mirror image of the other shapes.

ANSWER 215

10. Multiply the two numbers on the outside of each segment, divide the product by 1,2,3 ...8 respectively and put the new number in the middle of the opposite segment.

ANSWER 216

32. All the others have a partner, with the digits being reversed.

ANSWER 217

56. Take 2/3 of the number in the top left square and multiply it by twice the number in the top right square. Put the new number in the bottom square.

ANSWER 218

B.

ANSWER 219

C. All the others, when reflected on a vertical line, have an identical partner.

ANSWER 220

5. Add both numbers in one segment, add the digits of that sum and place new number in the next segment, going clockwise.

ANSWER 221

8. Starting at the top left corner add the first three numbers and place the sum below, beside or above the second number as appropriate. Moving around the square in a clockwise spiral, repeat with the next three numbers, etc.

ANSWER 222

B. Each column contains faces with 4 different types of hair, pairs of ears, eyes, mouths and face shapes.

ANSWER 223

C. A and D, and B and E are pairs. When reflected against a vertical line and turned, they are identical.

ANSWER 224

D and E.

ANSWER 225

141. The colors are worth Red 2, Green 4, Orange 7, Yellow 9. Multiply the numbers in each square together.

ANSWER 226

17. The colors are worth Red 6, Yellow 7, Green 10, Orange 12. In each square subtract the lower color from the upper. The colors represent numbers but are NOT necessarily under 10.

ANSWER 227

The pattern starts at the top right and goes in diagonal stripes from left to right.

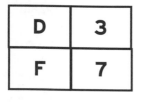

ANSWER 228

57, 71, 53, 45. The colors are worth Blue 3, Yellow 5, Orange -4, Green -5. Multiply the two top numbers in each square and add them to the product of the two bottom numbers. Then add or subtract according to the color of the square.

ANSWER 229

90. Colors are worth Orange 25, Purple 17, Yellow 36, Green 12.

ANSWER 230

The minute hand should be on the 4, the hour hand on the 8. The numbers the hands are pointing to are doubles of each other. The lower number moves forward by 1 each time, with the hands being reversed.

ANSWER 231

D. The formula is: left + (middle x right) = top + (middle x bottom), but in D, the answers are 26 and 25 respectively.

ANSWER 232

There are 43 pairs.

ANSWER 233

14 spotted tiles

ANSWER 234

410. In all the others the first two digits added equal the third.

ANSWER 235

54. The colors are worth Pink 3, Orange 4, Yellow 5, Green 6, Purple -2, Red -4. Add the value of the colors to the number in each square.

ANSWER 236

20. Left hand x right hand ÷ waist = head. Left foot x right foot ÷ waist = head.

ANSWER 237

Start at the top right and move in an anti-clockwise spiral. The dot moves clockwise around the square.

ANSWER 238

96. The colors are worth Pink 2, Yellow 3, Green 4, Orange 5.

ANSWER 239

A.

ANSWER 240

ANSWER 241

The formula is (right x left – top) x black fraction of circle = bottom.

ANSWER 242

625 and 5. The cubes of 7, 9 and 13 go into the right-hand circle, the squares of 18, 26 and 54 go into the left-hand circle.

ANSWER 243

C and F.

ANSWER 244

A. The edges of all the symbols in one square added together, increase by 2 with each square (i.e. 12, 14, 16, 18, 20).

ANSWER 245

7. Multiply the two numbers on the outside of each segment, divide their product by 2 and place the new number two segments ahead in the middle.

ANSWER 246

20. Take two numbers in adjacent circles. If both are odd, add them. If both are even, multiply them. If one number is odd and one is even take the difference. Put the new number in the overlapping section.

ANSWER 247

The hidden letter is F. The pattern is diagonal stripes starting from the top right and going up from right to left.

ANSWER 248

The pattern sequence is shown below. It starts at the top left and works downwards in a vertical boustrophedon.

ANSWER 249

 The pattern sequence is:

Start at top left and follow the pattern in a clockwise spiral.

ANSWER 250

27 or 729. The numbers are part of a sequence that alternates A^3, B, C^3, D, E^3, ...

ANSWER 251

F. Each shape changes into a shape with 2 extra sides. The order of shapes is reversed.

ANSWER 252

B and E.

ANSWER 253

11. Multiply the number of sides of each number by 3, and then subtract the number printed.

ANSWER 254

9. Multiply the two outer numbers in each segment, and divide the product by 2 and 3 alternately. Place the new number in the middle of the opposite segment.

ANSWER 255

56. (Head x left foot) ÷ waist = right hand; (head x right foot) ÷ waist = left hand).
(14 x 15) ÷ 5 = 42; (14 x 20) ÷ 5 = 56.

ANSWER 256

E. The squares with lines from the bottom left to the top right have arrows pointing up or right. Squares with lines from the bottom right to the top left have arrows pointing down or left.

ANSWER 257

D. The whole figure is reflected on a horizontal line. Any shape with straight lines is then rotated by 90° clockwise and a dot in a round shape disappears.

ANSWER 258

B and F.

ANSWER 259

G.

ANSWER 260

11. It is a series of prime numbers.

ANSWER 261

D.

ANSWER 262

91. All the others are prime numbers.

ANSWER 263

5. Three numbers in a horizontal line add up to the fourth number.

ANSWER 264

A. Multiply first and last digits. Subtract second digit for hours and add third for minutes.

ANSWER 265

D. The formula is: (right x shaded fraction of left) - (top x shaded fraction of bottom) = middle shape's number of sides. Therefore, in example D: (18 x $\frac{2}{3}$ [12]) - (12 x $\frac{3}{4}$) [9] = 3. The answer shape should be 3-sided, so it is the odd one out.

ANSWER 266

D. The symbols turn by 180° and 90° alternately. The circle and square swap places, the diamond and rectangle swap shading.

ANSWER 267

105. The colors are worth Yellow 4, Pink 5, Green 6, Orange 7. Add the value of the color to the number in each square.

ANSWER 268

19. Colors are worth Orange 3, Green 4, Red 5, Purple 7.

ANSWER 269

77. The colors are worth Purple 3, Green 4, Yellow 6, Orange 9. Add the left side to the right side and multiply by the base. This is Result 1. Now add the two upper internal colors and subtract the lower. This is Result 2. Then subtract Result 2 from Result 1.

ANSWER 270

34. The colors are worth Green 3, Red 4, Yellow 5, Purple 7. Add colors in each square together.

ANSWER 271

26. The colors are worth Red 3, Yellow 6, Purple 8, Green 9.

ANSWER 272

It will fall.

ANSWER 273

27. The colors are worth Yellow 2, Red 3, Green 4, Purple 6. Multiply the sides of the triangle together to get Result 1. Add the inner numbers together to get Result 2. Now subtract R2 from R1 to get the answer.

ANSWER 274

ANSWER 275

19. The colors are worth Orange 3, Red 5, Purple 7, Green 4. Add colors in the same square together.

ANSWER 276

28. Colors are worth Purple 5, Orange 2, Yellow 3, Green 6. Add colors in each square together.

ANSWER 277

The hours move back 3, 4, 5, and 6 hours. The minutes move forward 4, 9, 16, and 32 minutes. The seconds move back 1, 2, 3, and 4 seconds. The time on the fifth watch should be 21:14:51.

ANSWER 278

C.

ANSWER 279

A.

ANSWER 280

B. Billy's plot has the greatest perimeter.

ANSWER 281

A.

ANSWER 282

D. In all other cases the number of cross pieces on top of each vertical line is multiplied by the number of cross pieces on the bottom. All give even answers

apart from D.

ANSWER 283

D. Add a cross piece each time, alternating between adding them vertically and horizontally. A vertical cross piece changes the color of the arrow head.

ANSWER 284

D. The second hand moves forward 30 and back 15 seconds alternately, the minute hand moves back 10 and forward 5 minutes alternately, and the hour hand moves forward 2 hours and back 1 hour alternately.

ANSWER 285

D.

ANSWER 286

H. Rotate one place clockwise and then reflect across a horizontal line through the middle of the figure.

ANSWER 287

The third on the second column and the fifth on the third column.

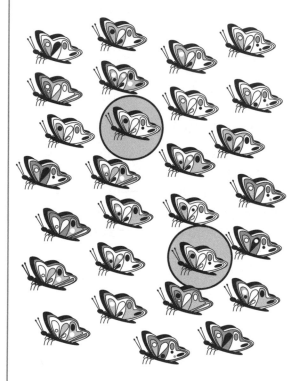

ANSWER 288

D.

ANSWER 289

D. Circle and triangle alternate. After a circle the next figure moves around 1 space, staying on the same side of the line. After a triangle it moves on 2.

ANSWER 290

Blue = 8; Green = 9.

ANSWER 291

1. Starting with 64, subtract 1, 2, 4, 8, 16, 32, missing a number each time and working in a clockwise direction.

ANSWER 292

A square. If the three numbers around the triangle add to an even number the shape is a square; if it is odd, then it is another triangle.

ANSWER 293

Penultimate triangle on the bottom row. Sequence, starting from the top and working from left to right, of dot, miss 1 triangle, dot, miss 2, dot, miss 3, dot, miss 4.

ANSWER 294

C. Curved lines gradually encroach on space within triangle.

ANSWER 295

D. One tip of the star is missing.

ANSWER 296

C.

ANSWER 297

F. Small square becomes a big square and vice versa. A small square with a triangle goes to small square alone. A triangle on big square remains a triangle.

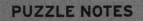

PUZZLE NOTES

PUZZLE NOTES